T0078082

iLove

iLove

SOPHIA N. SABER

ARCHWAY
PUBLISHING

Archway Publishing books may be ordered through booksellers or by contacting:

Archway Publishing
1663 Liberty Drive
Bloomington, IN 47403
www.archwaypublishing.com
844-669-3957

Written by: Sophia N. Saber
Edited by: KP Rose

ISBN: 978-1-6657-5555-9 (sc)
ISBN: 978-1-6657-5556-6 (e)

Library of Congress Control Number: 2024900810

Print information available on the last page.

Archway Publishing rev. date: 01/31/2024

Dedicated to my Mother, Nalah S. Renno

Paper has more patience than people.
- Anne Frank

CONTENTS

Chapter 1   The Beginning 1
Chapter 2   Homecoming 13
Chapter 3   Blue Balls... 21
Chapter 4   Like a Virgin 29
Chapter 5   Emancipation.. 45
Chapter 6   El Esposo 53
Chapter 7   MC.. 101
Chapter 8   Cocaine For Breakfast 115
Chapter 9   90210.. 157
Chapter 10   A Quick Bite 165
Chapter 11   Fourth Of July...171
Chapter 12   Mombasa, Kenya 177
Chapter 13   Back To School.. 185
Chapter 14   The Personal Trainer.. 197
Chapter 15   The Spaghetti Dinner.. 203
Chapter 16   You've Got Mail..211
Chapter 17   100 Days...219
Chapter 18   Thank you, next.. 225

Epilogue.. 233
Acknowledgements 235

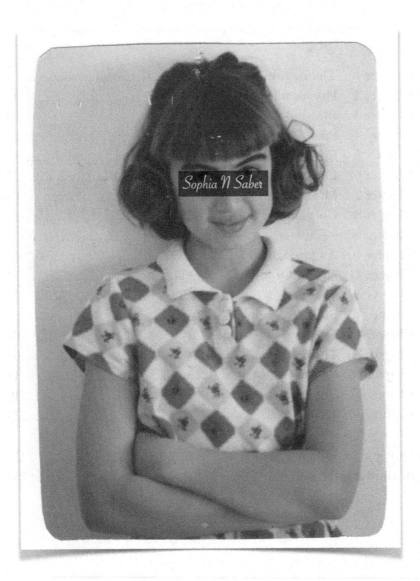

CHAPTER 1

The Beginning

Noun: the point in time or space at which something starts

This story begins on the first day of school in the third grade. I was nine. I wore a yellow dress striped with white. My hair was short. My eyebrows were thick. I had crooked teeth and an awkward personality. I attended an elementary school in the foothills of beautiful Boulder, Colorado. I lived in a trailer park with my father, who was raising us alone. I have one brother; he is younger than me by only 18 months, Irish twins, they say.

My mother lived in California and had no custody of us then, so my father was the adult in my life, and my little brother was my best friend. We lived a simple life; we rode our bikes to and from school and usually stayed in the YMCA program after school to wait for our father to pick us up.

He drove this old 1940-something Ford pick-up, which he had converted from a classic machine to an industrial work truck; it had large white panel boxes on a steel frame flatbed that he transformed into a high-power hydraulic dump truck. He would drive alongside us as we rode our bikes until we reached home. We would usually participate in preparing the inevitable dinner choices of Hamburger or Tuna helper. I would usually tear open the packages and boil the noodles. My father usually cooked the meat while my brother struggled through his homework at the table in tears.

I was the only girl living with two boys. There were often fights between us. More often than not, I felt outnumbered and completely misunderstood. I was missing my mother, who only had monitored visits and limited phone calls, and I was becoming lost, angry, and confused. However hard things were at home, school served as a joyous escape for me in those years.

I made a friend named Sophia. I didn't like her at first only because she had my name. Then I got to know her, and she quickly became my best friend. We did the usual things: sleep overs, listen to Ace of Base, and talk about our futures.

I had other friends, too. I even had a special friend, Jim Mallory. He was a blonde-haired, blue-eyed boy. We had been friends half the year throughout third grade, making our young romance an official thing around spring break. We played Pogs during recess, and he sometimes listened to me talk about my home life. Mostly, we liked to play imaginary games like house, a youthful version of Civil War reenactments minus the fantastic costumes, or our favorite, X-Men.

He was always Scott Summers, and I always played Jean-Grey. I loved playing her, with her telepathy and seductive nature. I was attracted to her character and embodied her as best I could, as well as the story I watched unfold every Saturday morning right after Animaniacs. Derrick played Logan, Bonnie played Gambit, Kyle played Beast, Morgan played Rogue, and Hattie was Storm. Some days, there would be substitutes. Since we all watched the same TV shows, we all knew the plot line, and subbing in was easy as long as you had watched the previous Saturday.

Eventually, our imaginary drama created real-life scandals. In the TV series, Scott and Jean break up, and Jean ends up marrying Logan. So, naturally, there was a wedding held on the wooden pirate ship in the schoolyard, which over 15 of our mutual friends witnessed, including Jim. He hated every minute of it. I kept telling him, "It is just a game- I am your girlfriend in real life!" He was not having it; he and Derrick never shook hands or played nice. As for the rest of us, acting out the game was more important than their jealousies. The show must go on.

Logan placed the cherry-flavored ring pop on my finger. We said

'I do,' and faked our kiss as the school bell rang. Everyone cheered, and we ran to our prospective classrooms. Jim and Derrick had an altercation that afternoon after school about whose girlfriend I was. I can't lie; I enjoyed the attention. I knew Jim loved me, and I loved him. He was my best friend to whom I told everything. Even though I was friends with Sophia, Bonnie, and Morgan, I was closest with Jim.

The foolishness eventually ended, and we all moved into Fourth Grade. Jim and I had such a good connection, that we remained boyfriend and girlfriend the following year. Fourth grade wasn't at all memorable for me. I turned ten that year and I remember I had requested my dad get me a cake that said Happy Birthday, Leslie; I was determined to rename myself. So, he did. The next few months, I would be Kim, from the Power Rangers, then slowly make my way back to being Sophia.

It was now summer '95. I was between fourth and fifth grade and wasn't sure what was next. For the time, Jim and I could keep our relationship alive thanks to the summer program at the YMCA. In summer camp we got day trips and more exciting stimulation like sports camps and juice boxes. They would plan little events and day trips for us so we didn't get too bored riding bikes in the parking lot next to a softball field, usually filled with drunk adults.

This particular day trip was to go see the new Disney feature film Pocahontas. Jim and I made a plan to have our first kiss on our first supervised group date. We decided on kissing when John Smith and Pocahontas kissed, and we executed our plan impeccably. We sat together in a row all by ourselves, with a row of our closest friends right behind us creating a human wall from the camp counselors who would definitely not approve of our plan.

The movie was exciting! Like no kind of animation we had seen before. We watched in complete awe as Disney got more creative with their characters and colors and animation. Pocahontas was a big deal. We sat next to each other holding hands and waiting and wondering if they would ever kiss. Finally, the tone of the movie changed, and the two characters met in secret under a waterfall. The wind blew turquoise wisps about the two who swirled in the confusion of love amidst tribal and cultural misunderstandings.

As they kissed in a whirlwind of Disney magic, Jim and I closed our eyes and mirrored Pocahontas and John Smith perfectly. It was as if we were kissing under that waterfall. There was nothing awkward or weird about kissing a boy, especially this one. I knew he was kind and he meant it and also that he loved me. Our friends all smirked in unison and as soon as the movie was over, asked a plethora of embarrassing questions.

"How did it feel?"

"Was his tongue slimy?"

"Did it smell funny?"

"How did you know what to do?"

"Are you going to do it again?"

We were the first to kiss out of the bunch. We were applauded and ridiculed all at once. I was completely satisfied. So were all of our friends. At home however, the volatility between my parents and I was growing. My father could no longer ignore the fact that I was suffering not being with my mom, it was profoundly affecting our relationship and the relationship I wanted so badly with my mother.

For the remainder of that summer I was focused on finding my way back to my mom in California. I began fifth grade that year at the same school and still with Jim. My father had agreed to let me visit my mother, unsupervised, and without my little brother. Thanksgiving couldn't come quick enough. I couldn't wait to tell my mom all about Jim and how close we had been for the past two years.

Being with my mother was completely different than being with my father. He was rough with me and expected so much, while she catered to my emotional and physical needs. After talking about Jim, she asked if I missed him and if I would like to call him. I had his number memorized and he had mine memorized, in case of emergencies. I was nervous, but agreed. If she called him with me, I felt like I could do it.

I was on the telephone in the kitchen with a cord attached to the wall so I couldn't move. Mom was on the other phone, the cordless one, listening in so she could guide my first stressful moment with love. The phone rang twice, and his father answered. I froze, so my mother began waving her arms, frantically mouthing,

"YOU NEED TO SPEAK!"

"he-he-hello, is Jim there?"

"Yes, one moment please, may I ask who is calling?"

"Sophia". I said with a trembling voice under buckets of sweat. I heard phone static as if his father had put the receiver to his chest to mute his voice. Then I heard Jim.

"Hello, Sophia, how's California?"

I immediately relaxed, just the sound of his raspy voice could put me at ease. My mom stood in the kitchen with the receiver up to her ear. She would smile and give me thumbs up every now and then; I remember her giggling and placing her hand on her mouth or shaking her head if I mentioned something embarrassing. She was the perfect guide. The call was quick, I just had to hear his voice.

After we hung up, my mother was full of new questions. She asked why I liked him and if I knew what having a boyfriend was. I obliged and told her all about him: his blonde hair with blue eyes and the kind of raspy voice that just drew you in; he was a great listener and was also funny. But for me, the main draw about Jim, what completely pulled me in, was his temperament. For a 10 year old he was so calm and collected. He was friendly with everyone, and everyone liked him. I liked that. He wore a red string bracelet on his right arm at all times. When I asked about it– or anything else– he shared with me. He was Buddhist and brought me a red braided bracelet to wear as well.

My mother seemed proud and she patted me on the back for my response. It was shortly after this conversation that my mother must have realized she would be sending me back to Colorado after Thanksgiving. She knew a girl needed someone or somewhere to dish all the details of her romances to, she just couldn't be there the way she wanted to be. So, we went to the Hallmark store in the mall and she bought me my first diary.

She told me to write everything down - good and bad. She promised that she would never peek, and that I should keep it hidden. I had never thought of writing before this moment, but have never thought of not writing since.

On November 27th 1995, I made my first entry.

Dear Diary,

Today I was with my mom at the mall. We bought a snoring bear for Adam and an arcade stick for my Sega genesis, and this diary. We had to return the arcade stick to KB Toys because we were not happy with it. Tonight we had my moms pork chops, peas, stuffing and egg nog. Then we played a trick on Adam. We waited for him to fall asleep then we put a super sonic snoring bear beside him and pushed the button on the bear and video taped the whole thing. Adam was not amused but we were.

This was the first time I felt the most powerful magic I would come to know. Writing. Something about a pen to paper, the way it would glide. The words would fill the space on the page and begin to swim like fish in an ocean; and with their swimming I could see they each had a life, a story to tell. Right then and there, writing became my best friend. I took to writing very quickly, and continued to explore the possibilities the pages presented to me with each new blank space. I began to look forward to those spaces daily and eventually I began to live to write.

11.28.1995

Dear Diary,

Today we went to the mall to get some new shoes for me and my mom. Then we went to dinner with SGM and SGP (step-gramma and grampa). We went to Red Lobster where I had the most disgusting spaghetti, but the cheese bread made up for it. I got to ride home with SGM and we couldn't find our parking ticket but then we found it.

11.29.1995

Now I only have three days before I go up in a plane with SGM. She's the pilot. I miss my boyfriend so much. Wherever he is please tell him I love him very much. To me a boyfriend is someone I can talk to whenever there is nobody else to turn to. I met him in third grade and we've been together ever since. Love him very much.

11.30.1995

Well today is the day I went up in a plane with SGM...(a few hours later) Well, so, maybe I didn't go up. I did have a long chat with my mom about my boyfriend. I think now I know more than I ever did about boyfriends, so now I feel much more secure about Jim. Now that somebody else knows about my love life, I am able to talk about him to my mother whenever I want to.

11.30.1995

Well, today I tried to get ahold of Jim, all I got was his answering machine. Oh yeah, in case you're wondering I did not get to go up in the plane with SGM there was too much

turbulence. Then we called for Jim, and his dad answered
and finally I spoke after my heart popped out of my chest.
But everything is ok now.

My mother had been married two times at this point, and was working on her third husband, Adam. I was young, but she didn't brush me off as a kid who didn't know what I was feeling. She knew I knew, because at my age, she knew she knew. My mother gave me the gift of writing and storytelling, and free therapy if I would ever need it. She also encouraged and passed down to me my sense of needing to belong with someone romantically.

I had come to visit again for Christmas and the New Year, since it was her birthday. She followed up with me about the progress of my relationship and my friends at school, she took me to buy new clothes, and to eat.

My time during the Christmas/New Year break was short-lived. It would be the last memory I have of my mother before her great mid-life change; a change that would take away the woman I had come to know as my mother, and replace her with an unknown.

1.1.1996

Well, right now I am leaving, and I don't really want to.
(I'm leaving my mom) I am on the plane back to Colorado
and I don't really want to go back. I want to stay longer, if I
had a choice I would stay with my mom. But I wouldn't let
her lie this time. I think I did pretty good on that, what am
I talking about? I've seen a whole new side of my mother,
a side I would love for my father to see. I love my mother
very much

1.3.1996

> *Today, I went to school. I am doing better not thinking about my mom at night. That's when I have the most problems because that's when we would have the most fun... Good night mom, I love you and miss you very much.*

1.4.1996

> *On Saturday I am thinking of asking my dad if I can go live with my mom for two summers and one year. Or until I want to come back. You see he has offered me to go live with her. So I am thinking of taking that offer.*

1.5.1996

> *Tonight I oopsily went too far. This time, tonight I yelled and yelled at my dad cause I want to live with my mom! I WANT TO GO LIVE WITH MY MOM!!*

1.7.1996

> *Well I got what I wanted. I get to go live with my mom. OH BOY I CAN'T WAIT! I'm going to quit 5th grade now and go live with my mom. YUPIE!!*

1.8.1996

> *MOMMY MOMMY I CAN'T WAIT MOMMY MOMMY MISS YOU SO MUCH MOM I CANT WAIAIIIIIIITTTTT!!!!*

1.13.1996

> *I had my 11th birthday party. I got lots of things, my mom*
> *ordered me a birthday clown. Who read aloud a note from*
> *her and I really started to cry.*

I was having a rough time navigating life without my mom. She had, in such a short period of time, helped me with what I cared about the most at that time, my boyfriend.

Jim and I began to have problems. My behavior started becoming erratic and complicated: I would break up with him and then we'd get back together. He understood and always accepted me back, but I had begun wearing him down.

1.25.1996

> *Well, I dumped Jim. I like another boy named Willie, I*
> *asked him out and he said no. He likes another girl. BUT*
> *I KNOW HE LIKES ME MORE!*

Jim and I had said our goodbyes summer '96. The summer between fifth and sixth grade was when I was finally able to convince my dad he should let me try Cali. Not with my rational words, but instead my erratic behavior and negative attention seeking gimmicks. I didn't leave the old man much of a choice; reluctantly, he agreed.

To my surprise, on arrival I found my mother had changed dramatically. She had accepted Christ and had become a born-again Christian, the Apostolic pentecostal kind. A rule-bound, scripture-following, holy-ghost-having, foot-stomping, isle-running, in-Jesus'-name-baptizing, "Hear o Israel the Lord our God is one!" type of Christian.

For as long as I could remember I had been seeking the approval, love, and affection of my mother. I saw this change in her as an opportunity for me to gain her love. I worked

endlessly to converge with her new behavior and lifestyle. I, too, became a born-again Christian.

9.23.1996

> *How ya doing? I gave my life to Jesus Christ my messiah and now I am happy. Now guess what? I am living with my mom and thank God for that. Ok, ok so I got something better than a diary. My holy ghost, my friendly companion. Well I should really get to sleep. Good night diary. Dedicated to my lord: Facita faghadabadassa fhathacita faghadabadassa (I wrote in tongues, that's how I pray now)*

10.5.1996

> *Dear Diary,*
>
> *Today I got into a huge fight with my mom. She wants me to be grounded with God, and I feel so bad. I feel horrible. It's one of the ten commandments to obey thy father and obey thy mother. And I didn't. I feel so awful... I love my mom, but I love Jesus more. Love, Sophia*

11.13.1996

> *Oh my dear sweet lord, I have not written to you for almost 3 months! But I have an excuse, see at school we made these other journals and we have to write in them for a grade so that is thee only reason I have not been writing in you, but for now I have to go it's late.*

11.14.1996

> *I'll have to write to you in the morning. Ok it's 6am here I am writing to you. A lot has been going on at school and*

everything. Some things are a big deal and some are not. Do
you mind me telling you about it? _____ no? Ok, I might
take a few sentences. It all started a month ago when Sasha,
Jesse and Ariel beat me up! They pinned me against a wall
and shoved me in a trash can. I didn't want to tell, but I did.
Since then I have been getting into and out of a lot of trouble.

11.17.1996

Dear diary,

My mom has really changed, she used to be so nice and now
she's just a witch! Always moody, I don't know what happened.

**My younger brother came to visit that Thanksgiving, we
were both with our mother, who neither of us recognized
anymore. He realized how disappointed I was that the mother
I had missed so much, in a way, was no longer there. I made
it through the end of that school year roughly. My mother
enrolled me in a private christian academy that was run by
our church. She would clean the bathrooms and do other
small favors to help pay for my tuition.**

**I was in a class of nine: three were in the sixth grade,
three were in the seventh grade, and three were in the eighth
grade. I honestly had no idea what the hell was going on. I
was bullied, and never fit in with that particular crowd, no
matter how hard I tried. But I did love the Bible, I loved God
and I didn't mind the torture. It was better than whatever
was going on at home with my mother and her now third
husband, who also despised the change she had made.**

**Ultimately though, things didn't work out. I was being
forced to learn religious rituals and ideologies before academics, based on my progress reports that were court ordered for
my fathers approval. My final grades would render my father
helpless, he demanded I return home to Colorado.**

Homecoming

Noun: an instance of returning home.

I had moved back to Colorado by the beginning of 7th grade to be with my father, and by then he had moved from the trailer park in Boulder to a house in Lafayette with his girlfriend and her daughter who is ten days older than I. Regardless of how that made me feel, my father was presenting a picture that might have been an opportunity to be part of a legitimate family, and without the construct of extreme Christianity. For the time being, I was happy to be home and after some time, I realized how much I missed my father and brother.

I was deeply conflicted by my mothers sudden change in lifestyle and new personality. Whoever she had become, we did not get along. And the change my father had gone through while I was gone would also be something that I just had to get used to. It was the choice between two evils. My dad had won that election. At the same time, my mother's and my relationship began to deteriorate quickly, and set into a pattern of love/hate.

Friday, August 22nd, 1997

> *Last week my mom rejected me. She told me I could never call again, so now Shawna is my real mom!*

I had lost my motherly reinforcement, completely. That

phone call devastated me. I knew it meant I was solely dependent on the support of my father and the pseudo family he had tried to create. He had replaced what he lost with my mom and I with this woman and her daughter. There was room for a son, but never any room for me. His girlfriend and I never saw eye to eye, and while I desperately wanted to believe that she could somehow be half the woman my mother was to me, she never could be. I was on my own in my thoughts, feelings, and my journey.

It was the beginning of my 7th grade year. I had started to recognize some of my talents and being the center of attention was one of them. So, naturally, I took drama as an elective, and that's when I first saw him. There he was, the class clown, the teacher had yet to arrive and Chris had everyone laughing uncontrollably. I sat quietly in the back watching him, I knew within seconds I liked him. It had been two summers and one full school year since I had had any sort of romantic involvement, so I felt nervous.

I caught Chris's eye easily. He would walk me to my classes, though he never carried my books- He was too cool for that and I liked this about him. Everyday he would walk me to my bus stop after school which was two stops away from the one right in front of the school, because I had acquired a few bullies; the pretty, sexy, popular girls, yah- those girls hated me.

I'm confident that at this point in my life Chris was a crutch for the pain I was feeling from home, and my social maladjustments. Chris was patient with this catastrophe of mine, he would take the time to walk me two stops away and we found a way to make out in the ditch behind 7/11 before my bus would come. Making out with Chris in the ditch behind 7-11 was just the thrill I needed to still feel alive, wanted and seen. In a way he kept me going.

12.14.1997

> *Dear self, that is a title I got out of another girl's diary. 'It happened to Nancy' it's sad, it's about a girl who gets aids. To get you all caught up, I am not apostolic anymore. And I am back in Colorado. Shawna has finally had enough of me, and this morning over breakfast she told my dad right in front of us we had to get out. He just bought a house across the street from hers. Since he was only going to fix it and sell it we have to live in the basement. In the smallest part of the house, there's just room for my brother and I. My dad will still probably sleep at Shawnas. Oh well at least we're next door to the Gomez family now, their oldest son Matt is so F.I.N.E.! I gotta get to bed and catch you later!*

2.17.1998

> *Happy new year, sorry I have not written to you for so long. But I have been really busy with school and everything. On my first semester report cards I got two F's that is a really bad grade, yes I know. Now I am grounded for a long time. Till my next progress report. Which is about 9 weeks, a long time to be grounded. The first four days my dad did not look at me, or hug me or say I love you. I almost ran away to one of my friends' houses, pretty scary right? Good night*

6.29.1998

> *Hey, sorry for not writing in such a long time. I love you so much, I just read a whole bunch of you and you really have helped me through so much. I went to LMS (Louisville Middle School) this year and at first my grades were very bad then they went up. I was also popular this year. I was in a mix of preppies and popular sexy people. My two best friends were Brittany and misty, but out of the two my main*

best friend is misty. I have really matured this year. I had a lot of guys ask me out this year, I refused most of them except Chris. I'm still going out with him. Anyhow I had to come visit my mother over the summer and that's where I am right now, in California. I'm just sitting on my bed waiting for Jesus to return. It's 2:30 am and I am back in church and with God. I'm even pretty popular out here too. They all say I am so much prettier and nicer, and more mature. I really like it because I am feeling much better about myself. Love Sophia N Saber

Nothing much happened over the summer of 7ᵗʰ grade, we did some traveling as a family to Yellowstone, South Dakota, and to Nebraska for a tour de corn palace. Which in hindsight, I loved.

11.13.1998

Hey, sup w/ you? Nothing much here! It is really hard for me to write in you. I am in 8ᵗʰ grade now, and loving it! This year, at the beginning of the year when I came back from California, those bullies I had last year are now my adoring fans..I don't know what happened there. Somehow all the boys in school like me, even TJ, Chris, Kyler, Pete, Erik, Jordan, Scott, Matt, Zach, and Jodi. That's a lot. I only like four of them. But anyway. Sometimes I just want to run away and die. I can't wear wide leg jeans called jncos. If my dad could just meet me even half way, let me wear makeup or have a boyfriend let me go to dances and parties I would do much better. But I feel so isolated and alone. I can only be a child once and I want to do some things the way my friends do. Damn it. Love ya Sophia N Saber

Monday, November 23rd, 1998

> *My brother seems like such a happy person and I am such
> a fucked up little piss-head!! My dad is just a fucker!!! He
> doesn't know how to raise kids!! He needs to go away from
> me before I run away and commit suicide. And believe me
> I will! I am not afraid to do it either! Love you- Piss Head*

**Piss head was a term I had heard my father's girlfriend call
me, so I believed it. I placed blame on my father for never
taking my side, and for putting me in this situation to begin
with, he knew more than anyone what I had been through, he
was supposed to know what I needed but he didn't, he never
chose to help me and I could feel it. I disliked him for other,
more juvenile reasons like; not letting me run rampant and
getting away with doing whatever I wanted to do: such as
wearing J'ncos, or make up, or letting me have a boyfriend.**

**Chris filled in what was missing with my father in the
affection he shared in our make-out sessions. I felt loved,
and wanted and if this was how I could get it, I would dive
straight into an addiction to romantic love and sex, and never
look back. Chris taught me how to kiss properly, and, inadvertently, how to deal with sexual pressure from boys. He
was ready for more each time we had met, and I was always
satisfied with making out.**

**Each time we found one another in the ditch we went
a little further. Soon, his hands were on my mosquito bite
boobs and my hands were exploring the pencil tip poking
from his J'nco jeans. Neither of us really knew what we were
doing. But we seemed happy with this exploration of our
young developing bodies. It had elements of secrecy, and
youthful desire. There was no way we were going to stop just
because my father wouldn't allow me to have a boyfriend.**

**I thought Chris was cute and I liked him, not the same
way I liked Jim. Jim and I had a unique bond, one void of**

sexual contact except one kiss. I never loved Chris, our bond
was built on something different, something more evolved.
Naturally, what goes up must come down and slowly Chris
stopped walking me to class and was spending less time
with me. When I inquired, he became so angry. Claiming I
shouldn't be asking questions like that.

One day, we were in our ditch, and I could tell we were
sinking. He said to me:

"I'm ready to go all the way."

"Absolutely not!" I proclaimed. I was shocked at the idea,
since my father did have serious talks with me at a very young
age. He told me all about boys when I was about 12. He said
they only wanted one thing- and that one thing was ok as
long as there was mutual respect and a clear understanding.
He said my first time should be for love and love only. He said
he knew the day would come and that he hoped I knew to,
of course, protect myself physically but also to protect myself
emotionally. He said he would love me no matter what and to
never let any man make me feel like I had to do something I
didn't want to do or he would kill them. And then he would
kill me for not following his rules.

Within a few seconds, I just had to ask myself. "Did I love
this boy?" The answer was no, so I said no. Then he got up
and left me that day without saying another word. The next
day, my bestie Misty came up to me all 14-year-old drama
queen-like

"OMG, are you like, ok?!"

"ugh, last time I checked."

"Even though Chris went all the way with Amber Thorne
under the bleachers at homecoming yesterday?"

My vision started going, it went straight to tunnel vision
and I started to feel a bit woozy. I felt my blood begin to
boil through my veins and my skin suddenly felt too tight.
I wanna burst at the seams, beaming red and green at the

seams with anger and envy. I wanted to turn into a she-hulk, find the new girl and ruin her. How could Chris do this to me? We had a friendship, we were just together yesterday! How could he be with another woman, and so quickly?!

I barely made it through school that day, slinking through the hallways from period to period, avoiding anyone who may know me. I walked myself to my bus stop in ocean rain tears. I was devastated, he didn't even say goodbye, I thought.

I came through my house door in tears, my father rushed to my side.

"Oh, Doter- what's wrong?"

"Chris cheated on me and broke my heart!" Then I collapsed into his arms in a teenage frenzy of emotional confusion. My father was confused as well, since this was the first he was hearing of an outright boyfriend.

My father held me briefly but long enough to subdue my tears. Then he said to me,

"Do you mean to tell me you were having sex with this boy? Even after what we talked about?"

"No?" I was completely confused by the question.

"Well in order for there to be cheating there must also be sex."

I had no idea, that I had no idea, what cheating actually meant. I didn't understand the complex nature of romance and sex yet, I was using adult words for middle school drama. I thought cheating was what Chris had done, and it was but to my father it was not enough to ground me. Instead, he told me I would understand someday and then took me to see Titanic for the 11th time.

CHAPTER 3

Blue Balls

Slang: Epididymal hypertension, which is thought to occur when you get sexually aroused for an extended period of time but don't have an orgasm or ejaculation.

10.7.1999

> *Well, a lot has happened since December 1998. I got sent out to live in California with my mom, my dad said my grades were too bad in Colorado and that it didn't seem to matter who I was with, my grades would be equally as bad with either parent. I attend Hoover Jr High in Merced, California. I'm doing really well. My best friend Sandy doesn't go there, she is home-schooled. Anyhow, my grades were really good all year, and I am popular. I also graduated from 8th grade! Anyway, it's time for me to go to school. I am in high school now, and my mom and I decided we would give home-schooling a try. I'll talk a bit more tomorrow about boys and church. Lots of love Soph.*

I turned fantastic fifteen, January 15th, 2000. My father had decided it was time for my mother to give it a go. I was developing issues that required a mother's attention. So at the beginning of high school, I began my ascent into adulthood in cozy central California. The same town I had spent my 6th-grade year in. The weather was so much hotter than Colorado, and the diversity of people was much greater.

However, life in California was nothing like what I remembered from the times I had visited my mother when I was younger. The town seemed to change along with my mother's drastic lifestyle. We no longer visited the same places, conversed the same way, or even drove the same cars. Her then-third husband had bought her a new one. She also dressed completely differently, and all we did was shop. The places we used to visit, like the arcade or movie theater, had somehow become demonic.

Still, I wanted her to love and accept me, so I found a way to keep her attention. I had fallen back in love with God. I was legitimately involved with God, the Church, and Christ; the whole culture. I went the whole way, believing I was doing it as an act of my own free will. Even speaking in tongues and trembling with the holy spirit at the altar felt real. It all felt real.

The extreme views my mother had adopted, and the stance she now took on the worldly, secular things, crippled my growth in magnitudes. She had created so much religious turmoil for me at home that my academic pursuits never improved or developed. She home-schooled me for a brief moment to try and implement more "God" into my education. That only lasted about a month into my freshman year.

My father was infuriated by my mother's home-schooling antics. He claimed it wasn't part of the court agreement they had made for her to have me, so he pulled me back to Colorado, where I attended High School—*a public* high school. I was developing as a young woman and I found all sorts of fun ways to get into trouble. I would sneak out of my basement bedroom window at night with my little brother in tow; this way, if I got caught, we would both get in trouble-softening my portion of the blow.

My poor little brother would sit and wait for me while I made out with my friend Andrew. This typically took thirty minutes or so, then we would walk home and check if the lights were on. If they were on, we were dead. If they weren't, then the old man was still sleeping, and we were in the clear. We never got caught.

I rarely attended school. I was struggling severely. My relationship with my father was strained, to say the least. The influence of his girlfriend's disdain, and the disruption I was causing in their "perfect" family picture, never allowed my father to see me clearly or manage my behavior appropriately.

One day, about nine months into my freshman year, my father came to my school and told me to pack up my locker. I was going back to California. We drove straight to the airport while crying oceans of tears in confusion and pain. I felt like he was throwing me away as if I wasn't his. I didn't feel loved by anyone. After we both had calmed down a bit, he said to me, "Doter, I love you, I do. But I can see that you are struggling beyond my control. You don't listen to anything I have to say, and you want your freedom so much. I feel that if you stay here with me, we will just end up hating each other. I am doing this to save us. Let's separate now, to be friends later."

And so he let me go.

It was May 16, 2000. I was now sixteen and settling back into my life in California. This was my last chance to be parented, and my only option at this point. To avoid the failures of securing the love of at least one of my parents again, I went to where I knew I could feel loved and accepted: the arms of some boys.

Monday, July 24th, 2000

> *Hey, man, so much has happened since the last time I wrote to you! Well, I went out with Darren- BIG MISTAKE! Andrew was, too!! But NE how, now I like Michael and*

man, I think he is the one :) Seriously, I've prayed about it
too! Well I'll let you go! Love, Sophia Saber

The only people I was allowed to socialize with were church folk. Darren and Andrew attended my high school. Andrew was also the Youth Pastor's son, I was into that. Darren was a senior while I was a freshman, I was also into that. Andrew and I dated for some time, but my mother didn't like him, so it ended quickly. My mothers approval for every person in my life was ultimate. If she didn't like them, then there was simply no contact with them.

Michael, up until this point, was by far the most memorable of all my loves. I loved him with such purity and power; I will never feel love the way I did with this first love. It's like the first toke off of a foiley you're never going to get the same high as your first puff. He was that pull into worlds unknown, the Aladdin to my Jasmine. When he looked at me, he did so with admiration and authority. Michael was older than I was–four years my senior. He had four other brothers and the most beautiful woman I had ever seen for a mother.

She was Latina, with long black hair, and a voice that commanded attention with the very obvious strength of a lion. She was raising five boys, and I had never met a woman I admired more. I knew nothing about her, yet she was always so kind to me. Even when I'm sure she knew I was in love with her second eldest.

Michael was a lead in the choir, and was cast as Jesus in the play during Easter. He was educated and loved by his parents, I could tell. He was what I wanted; he was who I wanted to marry and be with for the rest of my life. I wanted to have his children. He and I attended bible study together and gave glances during Wednesday night youth gatherings. Sunday morning and evening services were more of a fashion show than church. We had such a strict dress code, and it was so important how you dressed that we all took it way too seriously. Imagine getting ready for prom two to three times a week.

To be honest, I don't remember many details from our time together- more so, I remember how he made me feel. I recognize that this feeling has yet to replicate itself. I didn't record much during this time because my mother was such a spy. I wrote things in code (which I now cannot decode) or I had just planned on always remembering the essence of the situation.

Noticing that I had stopped writing was very painful, because it was my mother who had originally gifted me writing. Now it was evil to her. Something I had grown to love, and be quite friendly with, was now somehow demonic.

Michael and I, of course, found a way around it. We wrote each other letters every week, sometimes multiple times a week, for a short period of time. To this day, I have all of Michaels letters, and some of mine, as well as our mix-tapes in a box that I visit every now and then. I'm surprised I have them. One time, my mother found them and drummed up this completely ridiculous situation between me, Michael, and the pastor of our church. She had created so much drama that we stopped talking for a period. We eventually started again, but that was the beginning of the end for Michael and I.

8.17.2000

Hey, today was the most traumatic day of my entire life! The way I feel, or shall I say felt about Michael was different. Not love and not like somewhere in between. He called me today and asked me why my mom is calling over to his house? I can't believe it! I can't predict my evil mother's next steps! Now Michael and I aren't talking and I can barely stand the pain! My mom knows I want to move out, she's a liar! She always will be! Before I came back to California my mom told me on the phone all I would be doing was going to church and staying at home to do my school work. I can't survive like that! I'll die. I'm a kid and should be doing kid things!! I feel an enveloping pain inside. I'm in a big room, trapped in a glass box. They can see me, but I can't see them. I'm trying to get out, but the evil one stands there with a whip in her hands. She puts on a smile to the world, but beats the crap out of me if I try to move or get help. She slays all the mighty dragon slayers, but Michael has just gone to get bigger weapons. To save the princess in the box.

8.19.2000

Shawna asked me if I wanted to be emancipated today, no idea what it really means but I like the sound of it. Freedom from this madness!

Saturday November 17, 2001

Hey you =) How are you? I'm still breathing. I can't believe how long it's been since I've had you! So on Oct. 31st, 2000, my father came to visit us to see what was wrong. Because my mother and I had been having some problems. He showed up at the door, I knew he was coming but nobody else did. That night my brother and I left with him, we didn't tell anybody that we were leaving, we just left from the hotel in the middle of the night. May 16th, 2001, I came back to California.

I soon returned to California after break. Michael came back too. He came to my house one evening while my mother was out of town. I had Mariah Carey's, "My All" playing softly in the background. This was the first time we had ever been alone. For whatever reason, I was ready to give up my virginity. I was trying to set the mood so he'd get the hint that it was what I wanted to happen, even though it was

completely immoral and against everything we believed in as Christians.

He walked in and looked at me a bit perplexed. He had never seen me in pajamas before. What we were doing was wrong, and we both knew it. He turned off the music, took me in his arms, sighed, and kissed me on my forehead. I couldn't believe it. He had kissed me. We went into my mother's bedroom and lay on the bed beside each other, pretending for a moment that we were grownups, that this was our room, and that we could have sex.

All of those teenage hormones were built up with no way out. After moments of painful silence, he asked if he could give me a massage. I agreed. I removed my shirt with little hesitation and lay face down on my belly. As soon as he touched me, he abruptly quit and just left. It took me moments to realize what had happened but as soon as I did I felt rejected by what was supposed to be my only connection to love. I was hurt and deeply confused by his behavior.

I didn't let this stop me from seeking what I thought I needed. Around the same time, the pastor's youngest son, Conrad, had developed some feelings for me. My mother was more than thrilled about this. Anything to acquire status in the church, and what better way than to have your daughter dating the pastor's son? I had approval from my mom, and the prospect of a drama-free, all-inclusive experience.

With both our parents' blessings, Conrad picked me up around 7:30 pm on a Friday night with a promise to have me back by 10:00. We enjoyed the youth activities at the church and an after party at his parents' house. He drove me home around 9:30 pm, and we arrived early, so we parked a few blocks away in the lot of my Junior High School. We started to make out, and I immediately felt uncomfortable with this. I didn't know him, and my heart still belonged to Michael-this was definitely wrong. He grabbed my hand and placed it on his penis, it was hard. Then he pulled it out. It was the first penis I ever saw. He looked at me and said,

"You see that?"

"Yes?" I responded inquisitively. He took my hand and rubbed it on his balls.

"Do you feel those?"

"Yes," I said, slightly mortified

"Those are my balls, and if I don't release them tonight, they will turn blue and fall off."

"How do you release them?" I asked.

"You have to suck on it till white stuff comes out."

So, I did. I did what he asked in his cream-colored Camaro parked a few blocks from my mother's house. The alternative of going home wasn't any better in my head. The next day, I told my church sister what happened. She was not at all amused. She explained what blue balls were- and how he had tricked me. I cried and cried. I thought I had saved that man's life! Now, instead, I felt so foolish, stupid, and gross; so very gross. Of course, his plan was to tell Michael and destroy everything for good. That almost worked, except Michael knew that I really didn't know better.

I only saw Michael once more, and then he met his beautiful wife, Penelope. When I first saw her, I knew she was going to be his wife. I knew that she was the one he deserved and she was who God had sent for him. I let him go once I had met her. I cried for him for almost a year- silent tears to sleep and silent tears to wake. Michael forever has a piece of my heart that will always be unobtainable to any new suitor. Your first love is your most powerful, just like the first puff of something very addictive.

CHAPTER 4

Like a Virgin

Noun: a person who has never had sexual intercourse.

I attended high school in Merced for the beginning of my sophomore year. I was re-introduced to Christ, still wearing floor length skirts, still awkward as hell, and still searching to be loved. My mother was cruel at this point. Her long and hard bout with men had led her to her third divorce. The first being from a man she married at sixteen, the second was from my father, and now from Adam. Adam was a tall, geeky computer guy. A civil engineer; boring, bland, and replaceable. I never understood their love until I went through their divorce.

I always wondered if my mother ever loved Adam, or if he was just a tool. He was definitely a tool—a thing she used to get something she wanted. Or wanted back, I should say. Since my mother had lost us in the custody battle, there were strict rules she had to follow, by order of the court. The custody arrangement stated that she could only have part-time custody if she was able to provide evidence of a stable household. For her, this meant she had to work and have a partner who could help.

So one day at a time she began to build. For my mother, finding a man to financially support her was alway step one. She met Adam in Santa Cruz at a time when my mom was still her fun self. He was probably attracted to her beautiful smile and the way she kept sarcasm dry; it made her sweet moments sweeter. It was all or nothing with my mother. I'm sure he was taken with her, but my mother was very manipulative. She knew how to coax men into giving her what she wanted while making them think it was their idea all along.

She and Adam were married February 14, 1997. In 2001, after they had been married for five years, he had finally had enough of her money spending, bible thumping, manipulative ways, and divorced her ass. We were on the run, yet again, and I was just moving back to what was supposed to be stability. My mother and I moved into my Aunts two bedroom apartment in the heart of the city. It was small and crowded with my aunt, her daughter, Victoria, my mother, and I. We were constantly on top of each other fighting and living inharmoniously.

My mother and her twin seemed to dislike their own daughters equally, but my mother loved Victoria as if she didn't already have a daughter; so they had each other, and again, I was all alone in my journey.

Sunday, March 31, 2002

> *I know I let a lot of time go by (again) since November. A lot has happened (I left off on May 16th). My mom and I were living with Sister Elle, whom I loved very much. After a while, my mom and sister Elle started fighting. We moved out for stupid reasons. We moved into my Aunt's house. That, to me, was way worse. There was less room, and my aunt was really weird. I was being restricted a lot and for no apparent reason at all. So I started sneaking out at night. Then, one night I took my mom's car. I forget where I went. I think just around. Then I took my cousin~ BIG, BIG mistake. My mom and I started having problems. Things got really bad. One night she grabbed me by my hair and dragged me around on the floor. I got up and pushed her*

*off of me. My stupid ass cousin called the police. My mom
got arrested, that sucked! About one month later my cousin
finally snitched on me about the car. I was arrested, taken
to court, and charges were pressed. To top it off, my mother
sent me to go live in a crack house! To me, that was better
than being with my mother. A hell'o'lot better. Anything
is better than her sometimes. Then, from the crack house,
I finally moved back in with my mom. We started having
problems again, as usual. The cops were called. She kicked
me back out of the house and into the home of one of the
church families we knew. A fucking pain in my ass. By this
time, I had stopped going to regular school (Golden Valley).
I'm at an alternative school called Valley High. It's basically
for kids with no life at all. I'm just here because I couldn't
deal with school while I was dealing with my mother, you
know. So I had to go there.*

    *But anyway, about one week later, I moved back in with
my mother. We still kept having problems, so I was staying
with my aunt on/off. The whole reason for the fact was this:
My mom was dating some guy off of the internet. She wanted
her privacy on the phone. She did not want me hearing her
conversations. So, she made me sign up for the Job Corps.
It's a school for kids who couldn't live at home and also go to
school. I called my dad and told him that I had made up my
mind, I wanted to go to Job Core. Basically, just to get away
from this bitch. The people from Job Core came, interviewed
me, and said 'ok.' It will take 4-6 weeks to get in. Now,
I am just waiting on that. While I am waiting, my mother
is having me clean the school (ACTS Christian school).
It's a pain in the ass! Let me tell you, she will have me go
to people's houses, whom I don't even know, and have me
clean it! It's just endless. I don't even do anything bad here.
I'm a typical teen. So, I called my dad and asked him if I
could come stay with him until it's time for me to leave for*

Job Core. I hope that he says yes! If not, I am soon running away! Seriously, as you can see, I had a lot to deal with. To top it off, yet again, Michael is not in my life anymore, which makes me the saddest person alive. But! I found some-one else to do the job. I fell in love with this man, and he has taken care of me. He is great, but he really doesn't treat me all that well. But, then again he does. Yesterday I had a talk with him about [sex], and he was so sweet to me the rest of the day. He came to the play with me, and he even held my hand. Jameson- I am so in love with you, baby. I'd do anything for that butthead! Through all of my ordeals, he has been there for me and given me comfort in the highest of ways. I wrote Michael an email about him, but he never answered me back. I hope he does very soon.

Anyway, remember all that goddamn drama my mother put Michael and I through? Well, she is trying to do that with Jameson and I. That's the only reason I haven't told her about us. She wouldn't approve. Not only that, she would scare him away. To make a very long story short: I introduced Jameson to my mother at the play. Just so she could freak out and call his mom to ask her questions about us. I've met his mom and dad. I don't know what's happened since last night, regarding Jameson, but the play was very good! It was hard to watch it though. Too many memories, and of course, I cried. Hey- This entry is 17 pages long, so I am going to go now. Love you! <3/always Sophia N. Saber

This is my first "long" writing passage. I had waited so long to begin writing again, that I had to get everything out in one breath. Of course, one of those nights I snuck out with my mother's car- I went and picked him up. We had been good friends all year, and I was in a painful place with my mother- I needed love. I wanted Jameson to Love me. I knew he wouldn't hurt me. He was my best friend. Even if after

we were lovers our journey as romantic partners ended, our friendship wouldn't. Or, so I tricked myself into believing.

I snuck out on a Saturday night. That was usually the best time to go, my mother worked a night shift, so when she got home she was good and tired. Plus, we had to wake up at 6 am to pray and then get ready for church. I called him up, and gave him the breakdown. "Hey boo- I'm takin' the whip tonight, be outside around 10 pm. I'll flash my lights twice, and you get in." "Word up baby bird". I would take her car, park it at his house, then jump into his black 5.0 mustang that made him so irresistible to me.

We found ourselves driving around in the endless orchards of Deadville Planada. I had been talking forever, complaining about my mom, and even crying some. He always listened, and would shoot honest feedback. Finally, he parked, leaned over the console, and kissed me. He looked at me softly, and said, "Are you sure you are ready for this?" I was so ready. I gave my full consent. Before he continued to touch me, he said, "You know this won't mean much more than what it is." I repeated what it was, so he knew that I understood he was taking my virginity, in love and respect, but not partnership.

I was completely at peace giving this man that part of me. We slipped into the back seat, and he made me as comfortable as I could be in the back of a 5.0. He slid the condom out of his pocket and put it on, it was electric blue. I had never seen one of those before. It felt natural, good, and exciting. I felt like a grown-up must have felt. We both orgasmed, and that was it. I was now addicted to something much more powerful and dangerous than the simple affection I had become used to seeking.

We only lasted a few more months, but I spent the rest of that year in his bed. I enjoyed sex. Really enjoyed it. Throughout our shenanigans, he had inadvertently introduced me to one of my best friends, Daniel, whom I quickly adopted as an older brother. Daniel was the kind of guy who was larger than life. He was funny, outspoken, and his humor was based around sexuality. We had the best of times together. I would often ditch class and go hang out at his apartment, wreaking havoc, and then cleaning up my mess. I used to break into his house and clean it, for whatever reason; We developed such a brother-sister bond, it was incredible.

One night, Daniel was having a house party. Jameson and I showed up together- I was the youngest one there. It was one of my first times drinking, and I got shwasted right away. I ran upstairs to Daniel's room to pass out on his bed. The next thing I know, I'm having flashing feelings of euphoria and there's a strange ecstasy pulsating through my body. I look down, and see this beautiful, blonde girl eating my pussy. I knew this girl, we had class together.

She wanted me and I let her have me. I turned my head to the left in pleasure, and saw Jameson and Daniel watching through the crack of the door, their jaws on the floor. I was in an intimate moment, and they were looking at us like a circus act. I was so embarrassed and outraged. I immediately sobered up, and smooshed her off of me, to pretend I wasn't enjoying my experience. The church had clouded my view on homosexual activity, and I was ashamed that I was enjoying it. This was the beginning of the end, for Jameson and I.

Saturday, April 6th 2002,

> *I called Jameson Thursday night, after he left the first time. I called him around 1:15. His little party was over, and my sister said he could come over again. So, he came over, and stayed till 4:30am! We had __SO__ much fun. Jameson, Jenna, my sister and I. Just talking for a long time. It was so beautiful. Then, he finally had to go home, because he was leaving for LA on Friday for his birthday. I called him, and*

we slept on the phone for almost two hours. He is so cute, I think I am falling for him. I don't know what I am going to do for two weeks without him, let alone one year!!! I wish that he liked me the way I like him...he makes me so happy! =) Oh yeah...Elder Bill died on April 4th at 2:30am. Sad, very sad. His funeral is on Monday, and I wanted to go to Jameson's, but now I can't. Hopefully, I can do it Tuesday. But, anyway, talk later <3/always Sophia N. Saber

April 7th, 1983 (His birthday but it's 2002)

Written for Jameson Kendrick Goddard:

To see your smile, to feel your touch
At times, I feel this may be too much.
But then those things they call butterflies start to move.
And I realize I love what you're doin.

Is it possible to feel this way about someone?
Some kind of spell or trance— what have you done?!
How do you make me feel this way?
You leave me breathless with no words to say.

You took me in your arms.
And with your charm you healed what I thought could not be healed.
All those empty spaces now I know are filled.

I could get lost just staring in your eyes.
With you I could tell no lies.
Just reality you see— You make me feel so free.

With you forever and a day could I be,
If only you and I could be "we"
I'd kiss away all your tears and chase away all your fears.

If you would let me be me, don't think I'm she.
You hold on so tight and seem so confused when I am in sight.
Why do you keep me shut out?
With you in mind there is no doubt.
When all I want is to be let in.
I know what you're sayin— To there I've been.

To see your smile, to feel your touch
At times, I feel this may be too much.
But then those things they call butterflies start moving and
I realize I love what you're doing.

April 15th, 2002

I've tried and tried to figure Jameson out! He makes me so
mad sometimes! Like what happened on Friday. Today I
called him to meet him at Daniel's house. He came, but he
never seems happy to see me. Never! Daniel seemed more
happy to see me than him. I mean Daniel is cool and every-
thing, but he's too sexual and tends to be rude sometimes.
But, you know- he was complimenting my stomach— if
Jameson could just learn to do that, man I'd be feeling good
about myself. But, I feel like no matter what, I am not good
enough for him. No matter what I do, none of it is good
enough. I honestly don't know if he knows what he does,
or if he knows how to do it right, you know? Sometimes,
I really miss my freshman, Jameson. For example, I was
sitting on his lap and talking about how Emmy was telling
me, "Yeah, Jameson likes me, but once I give it up he won't
like me anymore. That once a guy sees that a girl has brains,
he won't want her anymore. She's not just pussy, now she is
coming with a relationship." What does Jameson have to say
to this? "Well, if you had brains I'd like you." Or something
to that effect! Normally, I wouldn't have cared, because I can
take a joke- you know. But, the thing is, I know that he

wasn't just joking! So I got really mad at him, and still am. But, I didn't show him that I was mad at him, what good would that do? None. He said he was just "joking". But, I don't think he was, he jokes around like that way too much! Then, when he was dropping me off, I don't remember quite what I was saying, but nothing for him to say this—

"I don't know what you are trying to do Sophia, but it's going to backfire"

"What does that mean?"

"I dunno... just sayin'."

"You mean like I'm too controlling?"

"Yeah, something like that." he says." What the hell?! I am anything but controlling! Anyway, I'm out, peace! SNSxoxo

April 16ᵗʰ, 2002

Hey, I went to Jameson's house today. (Big Smile =)) At first, I was mad at him, but he changed that quickly. I was mad cause Lesley, his ex, was coming over and he wanted me to hide!!! How dumb! That really hurt me, you know, but I took it to heart. On the other hand, I have been verbally abused by my mother for so long that I feel like I'm worth nothing. So, maybe Jameson is just 'with' me because I do put up with him. But then, I have to catch myself- maybe I am being too hard on him, you know?! Anyway- back to his house... He told me that he and Lesley went to Modesto to get a dress and she took him to Red Lobster. What the Fuck?! This was recently like back in February. He tried to make it sound so old. So yeah, he still talks to her. That kind of hurts me. Does this really make me control? Or normal? I think I need to talk to Lesley about this, but what the hell am I going to say? "Hey Lesley back up off Jameson's Jock!" HAHAHA you know?!

Well anyway, we made up and talked for about 2 hours about my childhood and stuff. About soccer, about brr-brr my imaginary pig, which I didn't tell him wasn't a real thing. That's fucked up. I will tell him on Friday. I don't like to lie to him. Anyway, he was pushing all the right buttons on me and we ended up ★ "Talking heart-to-heart" ★ and at the end I started crying. Something in me snapped, and I felt a big ball of emotion: love, hate, scared, and sad all at one time. Just writing about the feeling I felt makes me cry a bit. And not like a boo-woo cry, more like I need a shoulder cry. I don't even know where it came from either. It was a good feeling, but I hated it. It made me sad and scared, you know. He said to me "why are you crying?" Stupid me, all I could think to say was… "I just love you so much." It was silent for five to seven minutes, just looking around, up and down each other's faces for a reassuring sign of approval or redemption. For me, it was not found. He held me right, soothed me correctly. I don't think I was wanting or waiting for him to say "I love you" back, I just wanted him to know how I feel about him, that I care about him. I feel like today I gave him a piece of me that no one could ever get to… My heart. There is an icy wall built, that I put there, because of all the hurt and pain that has been instilled in me. But, Jameson- somehow, Jameson of all people, broke through that wall today.

My outlook on him and my view of him is totally different than it was yesterday. You know, something Michael couldn't even do. Yeah, he went to get bigger weapons to slay the dragon that guards the glass box that contains a now lifeless princess. But he is taking way too long, or he left, or something happened! But Jameson came already equipped with bigger artillery. I often ask him why we are not together, he'll say, "why am I gunna wanna be with a girl who I can't even ride around with?!" Bullll-mutha-fuckin-shit!

*There's something else going on. I want to know what is
really behind this. Well, good night for now. <3/ always*
Sophia N. Saber

*Having a heart to heart meant we had sex

Sunday, April 21ˢᵗ, 2002

*Hey you! I prayed to the holy ghost tonight. I needed it
so badly. I got my box from Sister Elle today, with all of
Michael's old letters in it. I forgot how much I really am
worth. I forgot what I am capable of getting relationships
wise. As much as I love Jameson, I think I am going to have
to say goodbye, unless he agrees to give God a try. I need a
man who loves God. I looked up fornication in the bible just
to see how far under I am, it's pretty bad. If God is what
I want, and I want to move on, I need to stop having sex.
Man, I really missed God in my life. I'm glad he's back.
Now, things concerning JobCorps. I don't feel the need to run
away from my problems. I need to face what I have done. If
this is where God wants me, here at the Montoya's (house of
refuge), then this is where I should stay. I think it is God's
will that I stay here in Merced. We'll see. I'm out! Peace!
<3/ always Sophia N. Saber*

Mine and my mothers relationship was out of control, I
had moved out sometime in December, to a Christian based
rehabilitation and foster home. It was run by an older hispanic
couple from our church, the Montoya's, who were looking
for extra income. My mother paid them a monthly stipend
to babysit me, while she pretended I was 18 and moved out
of my own accord. My father definitely wasn't going to take
me back and I turned down my mothers offer to release me
to the care of the Job Corps.

My home life was beyond a whole ass mess. I was lost

entirely, in a sort of developmental purgatory I had entered around the age of 12. I was afraid I would never find my way out, or be granted a chance to finally grow up. So, I forced it in ways I wasn't mature enough for.

Monday, April 22, 2002

> *How foolish of me to actually think I could say goodbye to Jameson! But, I did tell him how I felt and what God had to say about fornication. He was so open minded. I asked him if he believed in Heaven, he said "yes," "hell?" "yes," "God?" "yes," so I read him some scriptures. Romans 2:7-10. I think I love him so much, if God would save his soul and bring him into the truth. Well, there's my husband. You know- I'm excited to see what God can do! Then we went to the park for a walk. We walked up Bear creek for about one hour. I told him everything, things that NO one knows, NO one. He listened and was kind. A true friend- Well I'm sleepy. Goodnight. <3/ always Sophia N. Saber*

Tuesday, April 23, 2002

> *Yo! Yo! Yo! This one will be short and simple. I went to Jameson's after school today =)*. Nothing bad happened today, just the usual giggling and playing around. At four-ish, I asked him to take me to atwater to get a watch battery. He did, it was nice. Then we went to Mario's. Hahah he had the hiccups and then he spit up! It was so funny! Anyway, I'm out! Peace. <3/ always Sophia N. Saber*

Wednesday, April 24, 2002

> *Hey this is the longest that I have written to you in so many consecutive days! I'm so sick of his bullshit! Friday was it! He friggin ignored me! OK I did not go over to his house*

just to be ignored! you know! One of his friends calls and he is on the phone from like 1-4ish! While I'm there the whole time! So I have not called him for a long time! Maybe never again! If he really cares he can call me! -SNS

Thursday, April 25, 2002

Hey! I called him from Toni's house today to talk to him. Or to go break up with him, you know. He didn't even care! I'm so heartbroken!...Hopefully he will call me tonight. I gave him my number, we'll see. I'm out. Sophia N. Saber

Monday, April 29, 2002

Guess what happened... Yup you guessed it! Jameson asked me out!!! I'm so happy! I have a boyfriend!!!

May 1, 2002

Happy May day! Hey, I am so happy! I feel like Jameson completed something, I don't know what, but I just have this feeling! I saw Montana tonight in church. He's so fine, he says he likes me. Ugh! Oh well too bad for him, I am already taken! -one SNS Xoxoxoxoxoxoxo

Monday, May 6, 2002

Hey- All my life all I have ever wanted is just to belong to something, to someone, somewhere. I don't really belong anywhere. I feel so alone, cold, distant. My mom came and picked me up from school today. And spit fire at me literally. When I got in the car she was trying to talk to me. I completely ignored her. Then she looked back and said this.

*"My God you look like Satan himself!! My possession
at its worst!! You slut! You think you look so cute don't
you?! Slut…"*

*I don't know what I did to deserve this, I guess I was just
born!? Fuck man. To top it off, I don't get to see Jameson till
Wednesday. But he wants me to go to Modesto with him.
He is so cute, let me tell you! He's all, "hey, you are going
to Modesto with me on Wednesday." I was all, "Hehe, ok!"
He is so cute! He is just going to pick up his turbo, but I
LOVE long car rides with him!!! Then just as I thought
my day couldn't get any worse…it did. I just moved into my
room and it is soo cute! Star is back, and I have to move back
into Christines room. This place gets on my nerves!*

-one SNSxoxo

Sunday, May 12, 2002

*Hey, just to keep you all updated, Modesto was fun, and
today, my mom called and wants me to move back in with
her. When will it all end?? When? -one*

**Shortly after the incident at Daniels house, with the beau-
tiful blonde, I mustered up the strength to break up with
someone whom I had obviously bullied into a relationship
with me. Even though I was repeating the words he made
me say the night he took my virginity. I wanted our love to
be tangible, it just wasn't.**

**I lived with the Montoya's till school finished that sum-
mer. I had been attending a continuation school in the valley.
I never actually stayed, I went for roll-call and left, usually
to Daniels, or to act out this drama that gave me a real sense
of purpose and control.**

I didn't feel I could make it any longer with the Montoya's,

so I ran. I was picked up, then ran again, and picked up again. I ran one last time... I wouldn't fail on my third attempt. That's when my mother agreed to legal emancipation. I only needed the signature of one parent, and I got it.

CHAPTER 5

Emancipation

Verb: the fact or process of being set free from legal, social, or political restrictions; liberation.

I was being tormented by the religious conflict I felt regarding the morality of my sexuality, or what I had come to know of it. I was missing a mother, not necessarily mine, just having a woman help guide me. And also mine. She had at least started my writing habit, and my writing is what helped me the most. It was my only outlet.

June 5, 2002

> *Hey! So much has happened in one week! Last week, on Sunday, Monday, and Tuesday, I had a fever of 103. That is a high fever, but I went to school Thursday. Well, not really. I went to Daniels to see Montana. See, we talked for a long time. I like him. He said this to me, "Before we get married." WHOA! He scored major brownie points right there! We had a huge water fight! It was the most fun ever. It was just Daniel and I. Montana just watched. But he still got soaked! Haha. Friday, I went back over there, and decided that I like Montana too. I guess he really likes me. He has such respect for me. I don't have to be some bad girl for him. He wants me to be a good girl for him. He wants me to be his. But he is SO BAD! I don't know if I could hang with that, you know? But I can be a church girl around*

*him. I can be myself. I feel so strongly toward him. He al-
ways pays me compliments, and I feel that maybe I've met
my match. Anyway- I broke up with Jameson on the 4th.
I mean honestly, we're better off just friends. But anyway,
I'm gone.-one Sophia f. Carey Plus, I got a new baby kitty,
Chastity May Morgan*

Friday, June 7, 2002

*Hey there, you! I saw Montana tonight. I really like him. I
couldn't sleep at all last night. Around 2:30ish, I was wor-
ried. I talked to him today, it turns out he was running from
the cops. I guess that's dangerous. We talked and decided
that when he gets back from Colorado, I will be his Lady. I
better hear from him tomorrow. And the next day, and the
day after that, and the one after that. But did I move too
quickly from Jameson?! I hope he's not hurt. I'm not. I think
we're better off being friends anyway. I think Montana is
cool! He's hella fine, too. Anyway- I'm gone -one* Sophia
N. Saber xoxo

Thursday, June 13, 2002

*Hey! Montana and D-drop never made it to Colorado.
They got pulled over, D-Drop went to Jail in Nevada, and
Montana is with his Mother in Sparks, Nevada. He calls me
every day. I've called him, too, from my sister's phone. She
is going to kill me. But we talked for a while. Maybe he's
the one. We both need work, but we both can admit that. So
it's all good. I miss him like crazy! I'm thinking of taking a
road trip to go see him. But we will see! I'm out <3/ always*
Sophia N. Saber

Sunday, June 16, 2002

Happy fathers Day daddy! Hey, I haven't heard from Montana for a minute. But that is the least of my worries right now. I chopped my hair off, I feel so cold, and alone. -SNS

Sunday, July 7, 2002

Hey you! Montana and I are official, as of July the 4th. Awwww. My favorite holiday, besides May day. Yeah- I know, we're cute. I went to Great America with Conrad. I got on the Drop Zone with him, and he comforted me. I'm too lost! Like, 50 guys like me, right now. It sucks. I really like Montana, but I dunno, Conrad has points, and Garret is coming back. xoxo

Monday, July 22, 2002

HAPPY BIRTHDAY PAPA!

Well, man, what a night last night. I was supposed to spend the night at a friend's house, but plans changed. Jenna and I went to Izzy's house first, got high, then went to the fair to try and find her cousins, Steve and J-dig, we didn't find them so we got a ride to Dennys & Walked out on our ticket. We were walking just fine till I spotted a cop and booked it! Jenna got away but I was cornered in an alley. I was caught and arrested. It was the scariest thing in the world. They took me back to Dennys and called my legal guardians, the Montoyas, to come pick me up. They came and got me. I was grounded for one month, meaning no phone either. I miss Montana. But anyway- what a Day. <3/always Sophia N. Saber

I had not been living at home for almost a year. I was living with strangers who obviously didn't love me and taking on the persona of my new love, Montana. He was a thug. He banged for the red team, and I didn't mind. I liked the danger, the mystery, the rebelliousness. It was a breath of fresh air. He made me feel like I was part of something.

He was short and handsome, always wore baggy pants with a red bandana hanging out of the right side. He had a swagger when he walked and talked. He made me feel light, like I was the good in his life. This is how we bonded— he was saving me from the death my mother was putting me through.

I met his mother and sister and instantly became a family member. His mother loved me the way a mother should love a daughter, and his sister and I became besties. She didn't care for my religious attitude, but if her brother loved me, so did she. Her name is Diamond, you know, like a Marquis Diamond. She is beautiful, and has the strongest personality I have ever come across. His mother was kind and motherly, she took no bullshit from anyone. They cared about me immediately, and mama even went to bat for me in the court of law against my mother.

Over the summer of 2002, I had legally emancipated myself from my parents. I saved up $1000, had a bank account, and a plan for the judge. My freedom was granted and I was free from my mother. I could make my own decisions, and best of all, I didn't have to finish high school. Fuck that.

I was in-love, exhausted from the continuous movement created by my mother and father, and I just wanted to make my own decisions. School was not in my plans, so I started working immediately. Mostly for my church sister at her in-home daycare that she started in 1999. I was her guy. Everything I know about raising babies comes from her. The most important thing though, was that now I was free. I got

the independence I had craved my whole life. The rest would fall into place.

Saturday, November 16, 2002

> *Hey there, long lost friend! The one place I can lay all my truths! Montana and I have been official for four months now. I have been to Reno and back four times to visit him, and I'm probably moving up there.*

Wednesday, November 20, 2002

> *Hey there, you! Well, diary, after all these years— this entry means so much. In this diary lies all the truth to my mysterious life. You know, every guy that I ever truly liked, and that truly liked me back, has said the same thing to me. "Sophia, I know you so well, but you're still so mysterious to me." It's weird, I hear that one a lot. In a way, I loved it, and in a way, I hated it. But now, diary, I'm at a point in my life where I'm not worried about boys. I have found a man. No more Michael/Conrad situations. I've chosen "the one," yah weird, huh? We're making a pretty big move this week. See, we're moving in together. We've been together four, almost five months now. Friday, I told him I'd be out there, and I will be. You see, we fight, but it's almost like both of us need to fight to survive, so it's ok. But anyway, I feel like this is my turning point from a girl to a Woman, but I don't know if I'm being a coward or not.-one*

Sophia N Saber xoxo

I want to say around October 2002 I made the move to Reno Nevada. I moved into Montana's mother's house with Diamond and all of our puppies! I was in love, not just with Montana, but his family. It was just what I had been

searching for, a sense of belonging to something, somebody, somewhere.

I was working at the mall, doing different jobs. Clothing retail, nose piercing Kiosk, you name it, I worked it. I hated it all. My life with Montana was fast-paced. He was an aspiring rapper and lived the lifestyle. He was ok. I didn't understand what was going on most of the time, but I played the part of a gangster rapper's girlfriend the best I could.

Wednesday, December 25, 2002

> *Dear diary, how are you? Good?! Well, me, too! Montana and I are still together after all this time. Five months going on six. Today is Christmas. He got me a ring, no strings attached. Just a beautiful diamond flip ring. One side is this beautiful diamond North star arrangement, and the flip side is an Opal. It's the most precious thing I have ever gotten. I will hold that ring near and dear to my heart forever! My Daughter will hold this ring near and dear to her heart as well. This Christmas was wonderful. -SNS*

May 1, 2003 (My second favorite holiday)

> *HAPPY MAY DAY! So I have a boyfriend, Montana (still), and did I get flowers? NO! I've been reminding him everyday to get me flowers today, did he remember?! I'm sure he did. He just didn't want to stop playing his video games to do something nice for me! Forget nice, anything at all would be lovely! A compliment- anything! For example, it's 10:30 at night right? I haven't seen him since I left this morning to walk Sativa, our dog. That was at 12:30pm. I got back and he was right where I had left him. Playing his video games. He actually just got done, but you know what- that's ok. I am not going to say anything. Not anymore. When the time comes, he will finally get how I feel. He may get it*

now and just doesn't care. Well anyway- I'm done. Love ya Diary.<3/always & forever Sophia N. Saber

Our fighting had escalated. Montana started using his hands and physical strength to get his point across. I would spend the next four months of my life in a physically and verbally abusive relationship. I kept telling myself that he had issues of his own- I knew he loved me, but eventually our differences got the best of us. I decided that I couldn't take being hit on any longer.

I packed my 1986 Honda Civic full of all my shit, drove to his job, kissed him goodbye, and just left. I left my dog too. I had been waiting for the right time, and this was it, this was my opportunity. This was how I ended my first year of freedom, by saving myself. I escaped with only minor injuries from physical abuse. Praise be to God.

El Esposo

Noun *a married man considered in relation to his wife.*

I had moved back to Merced in July of 2003, one month after I was supposed to graduate high school. Instead, I was driving home from Reno with my car packed full, blowing blue smoke out of my tailpipe, crying till I couldn't see straight. I had to pull over more than a few times to clear my eyes and to put water in my coolant system. However, nothing was going to keep me in that situation any longer.

Wednesday, August 12, 2003

> *Hey, Montana and I broke up. I moved back to Merced. We broke up at the end of June. We still talk, but we always fight. I still love him. I just can't put up with his shit right now. I am in between a rock and a hard place. I am homeless- I can't get my life straight. I don't know what to do. I'm lost! Ugh, anyway- I saw Jameson tonight. He's doing cool, I guess. I miss him. We're gonna hang out more often, hopefully. Hopefully. Life sucks right now. Big time. Big time. Anyway- I'm out. -SNS*

It seemed life had beat me, and I was exhausted. I was 18 now and completely drained. I didn't talk to my mother anymore; communication with my father was limited to sporadic phone calls. My only option was to drive straight to my sister's house. She had wired me some money to get back. I hadn't told anyone the details of what I had been through recently. I was just glad to be away from that whole situation.

I was living out of my car, couch surfing between my sister's house and random friends with whom I had grown accustomed to partying —the wrong crowd of course. We were into all of the wrong types of new things. I was introduced to crystal meth by one of my best friends. I grew up in the church with her. I felt safe somehow with her. We became addicted, and this addiction lasted for some months.

Twisting and toiling along the dark path this particular high took me on, introduced me to parts of myself I would have otherwise not known. During that period, I felt like I was awake, writing for months on end. We would all get high, and I would sneak off to write. Most of the time, I was in a bathroom on a toilet with a single bulb blinking above my head. I didn't care, I just had to know my words in that state. I did, and it was all garbage.

Something about that particular high and the environment made me reclusive. Still, in that disorientated and anti-sober frame of mind, my writing practice assured me that I did indeed have a special, unbreakable bond with a pen and paper. I didn't party high, I didn't drive or go out really, I just smoked my rocks and wrote my words. I also did a lot of cleaning. This phase didn't last long, though. I had started a new life pattern of saving myself. This would be my second major save.

I noticed what was happening to my body and the bodies and minds of my friends with whom I was hanging out. We were all changing, and it wasn't in a good way. I was skinny, probably a little smelly, and always hungry but couldn't eat. I knew that it was a slow death I was asking for, if I didn't move away from that addiction.

It was difficult to get away from it, to quit cold turkey. I did it, though. I asked myself– is it *you* or this pipe? I chose me. The descent from crystal meth ends in fights with your friends, with the demons in your head, the complete emptiness inside, and the physical failure of your body. I was in such an emptied frame of mind I can't clearly recall how I escaped; I just know I did. I did what I had to do to survive.

Shortly after I felt confident I had moved away from that addiction, I moved in with Daniel. He had a small studio apartment in the Northern part of town. He and I had gotten close since I had been back. He got protective over me, since he learned of the situation that unfolded with Montana. Since he had introduced us, he felt some sort of responsibility for it. We were the best of friends. More than friends. I saw him as my older brother, and loved him as such. We looked out for each other. I would make him get up early and walk to the gym; he made me bag up the weed we sold—a well-rounded, symbiotic relationship. I finally had a stable place to live, and I was developing a different routine that would land me in the presence of the man who would become my husband.

Monday, December 23, 2003

Hey you! Guess where I am at! Yup, you guessed it. Colorado. It's so weird to be back home, like a real home! I've spent most of my time in my room. Ironically, that's where I spent most of my time as a kid, too. Haha! Anyway, I saw Tractor Russ and Kathy today. I saw other people, but they are not important. Anyway ~ Daniel text messages me like I don't know it's him. He's trying to be Alejandro. Anyway, so then Alejandro texts me from his dad's phone. He ends up calling me, and we talk for two hours and 57 minutes. It has been a long time since I was able to talk aimlessly to someone. Alejandro makes me feel good. But the thing I like most about him is his wisdom. He has the potential to be a very wise man. He reminds me of my father. He has no idea that some of the small insignificant things he does are the most important things I look for in men. He's a real man, and I can really appreciate that he seems like someone who can control my angry little heart, just like my Dad. Not even Montana could do that. That's probably why he started hitting me. Anyway, I see beautiful things all day, and I'm constantly thinking Alejandro should be here to see this. I can't say I'm in-love with Alejandro- but I do love him. I am definitely going to let him know in every way possible. I want him to see that I can be his woman, the one he needs. I can't force anything on him, he knows. I've told him. Now, I am just waiting. If I have to wait 5 years, oh well. I have all I need from him now. I'm his mistress now I guess, it's kind of intriguing and exciting. I don't want to rush things. He is about to have a daughter. Wow- that's weird to say. Anyway- I'm tired, good night. Love Always Sophia N. Saber xoxo

Wednesday, December 24, 2003

3:43 a-mutha-fuckin-m! I can't sleep! Alejandro is on my mind. You are who I turn to in my times of need. So, here's the wrap… he texts me tonight- little does he know, we texted each other at the same time. I texted Daniel and said, "Goodnight boys…I love you.". Anyway- he sent me a text that said "U2? Me2!, I have my sister's phone for a little while". So I tell him to call just cause it's quicker. It was something about Marisol. I thought, man, this mfcka is slippin. So we cut shit short. I did the, "prove it," and he said, "mama, it's me." He has no idea how that feels. He says during sex. It makes me feel so good and special, like I have a chance. Haha! That's another thing you don't know about him. My chances with him are slim to none. We're both Capricorns, so we're both goats. Meaning, we're constantly challenging each other. We need to be challenged.. He teaches me things, like my dad. When I ask him questions, he answers me, even if it's two hours later. He might be busy at the moment, but that's ok. He rarely ever ignores me or blows me off. Alejandro listens to me. All the time. I like and respect him to the point where I almost think he could be the last person to me. But, I'm not sprung on him, nor am I in love. I love him as a dear friend and appreciate his friendship. Are there more feelings than that? Most definitely! Come on! I'm, you know- I won't allow myself to commit in my head. I already have, but not totally. To me, I am with Alejandro. I'm sleeping with him, so I'm with him. I knew from the beginning that his girlfriend (yes, I did just say that!...I know!)Marisol was pregnant! Wow, what the fuck?! I'm not too sure why I thought this was ok. Do you have any idea how incredibly guilty I feel? I respect Marisol. She got Alejandro, and she chose him. Yes, she trapped him, but there are two sides to every story! The point is, she loves him a lot. I don't know if that love is two-sided. I can't tell. If Alejandro stays with her, I will be surprised. But, if he is happy, then I will be fine. I could totally let him go and still be friends. I don't need Alejandro to be my husband. Just my friend. If I could sleep with Alejandro for the rest of my life, I would. But, someday, if we never take off, he will find someone. He is too good of a man. We could stop and be friends. By the way, I am super blowed. I couldn't sleep, so I smoked some of the weed Alejandro gave me before I came out to CO. So yeah- I'll probably wake up and read this and be mad that I spilled my real guts on paper. I'll just hide you better. But that's not something I want to tell anyone. It's just a girl drama, so I will keep it to myself. Alejandro knows, and that is all that matters! And with that, I am off to bed. Goodnight! It's 4:16 am Sophia N. Saber

Friday, January 10, 2004

Hey! Happy New Year! 2004! Yippee! Hey, ok, something is wrong with me. Sometimes I wonder! I cried in front of Alejandro last night. Not just, "cried." I was hurt. My walls came down! Ok, yah, I like Alejandro, but come on! This is starting to get scary. I am lying here next to him. He is dead asleep. He's so beautiful to me. His body hits home for me. You know- when he saw me crying, all he said was, "quit crying." Of course, he is still somewhat of a gentleman, so he asked, "Sophia, what's wrong?" "Nothing." I couldn't tell him. He doesn't understand my pain yet. He just wouldn't get it. But yah, something in me has been changing. I have had this weird conscience. I have not been feeling like doing bad things. Anyway, yah, my stomach hurts, as usual! I need to quit smoking! FUUUUUCK! I cannot think of one thing. Alejandro has sex on my mind. If everybody felt the way Alejandro feels, our world would be so happy. His face is the face of the man I love. That says it all. He is beautiful.
Sophia N. Saber

February 4, 2004

Dear Diary, man my mind is so doubtful and dramatic. Alejandro said he would come over last night. He didn't. He didn't even call. So, in my mind…OMG so many things were thought of. He told me he was doing something with his uncle. Little did I know, he was at Lamas with Marisol. I don't know why it bothered me so much, but it did. I love him. I wish I had never used that word before, but I did. I loved Montana, but not like this. I don't quite know how to explain my love for Alejandro, but it is true and deep. I wish I could tell him, or someone for that matter. I'll just keep the truth here where it belongs, in my heart and on these pages. So, on Saturday January 31ˢᵗ, we snuck off to the snow, just him and I. Well, and my brother and his friends. The ride up there was so ahhhh...I got my little brother high for the first time. Alejandro interacted so incredibly well with him. You have to have patience when dealing with my little brother. He did, and they got along. My mother even likes Alejandro! Anyway, just like when I was little, and my father and his girlfriend used to give us walkie talkies to go off on adventures, he, too, gave the kids walkie talkies. We climbed atop the mountain, found a spot, and smoked a blunt. It was romantic but not in some sort of sappy girly way. I swear. If I wasn't already in love before, then this is where and when I knew I was head over heels in love with this man. Alejandro Gonzalez Jr. I have never felt feelings like these before. He brings out the woman in me that I should be. He completes me and fills all my voids. He is the man. No Fuck that, he is MY man. I am so scared to lose him though. If he truly didn't love Marisol, he wouldn't even be with her. I know she is a good woman, and I know she is going to be a good mother. So, who the hell do I think I am trying to take her man?! Like I always say, you can't steal what wants to be taken.

Love always, Sophia N Saber

Alejandro and I do fall deeply in love with each other. He officially professed his love for me one night while high on ecstasy. I was so caught up in my euphoric world that I had yet to notice what was being said, or when it was being said. Drugs and sex (lots of sex) were a big part of the beginning of our relationship. However, there was NO doubt that he was my best friend; on-and-off drugs, before-during-n-after sex.

Friday, February 13 2004

Hey there you! I told you so! Ali snuck me into his house again last night. I slept so well. It's him, but just seeing his face first thing in the morning is the most wonderful feeling in the world. Anyway- at about 10:30/11:00, Marisol shows up! Now, I am laying naked in Alejandro's bed. So, he quickly hides me in his uncle's room, and lets in Marisol. Oh, My God!!! I hear him say, "Are you still mad at me?" "No." HA! I knew it! She really wants him! Oh anyway- It's funny where I found him & how I found him, and no one or nothing will get in the way of my feelings for him! Sophia N. Saber

Thursday, February 26, 2004

Hey there you! Alejandro finally did it. He lied to me. He had his friends lie to me, too. I've become a psycho~ he had my money, though. I don't know how to feel. If this is it, then he can kick rocks! As far as I am concerned, this is bullshit! I am his friend, not his girlfriend! You know what, lately, I have been feeling like being alone. Or that I don't want anyone around me, you know. Maybe I'm too weird for this world. Somebody, please tell me! Please help me! Does all this falling in love matter?! Nobody could love me the way I love me. Goodnight -Sophia

I had begun to wonder about love in a more substantial way. From all my previous crash and burns, I was beginning to wonder if love was even worth pursuing. Or if the *idea* of love was what I was pursuing. I was justifying and compromising myself at major turns, and would boil over when things got out of hand. I wanted to give him the cow before he bought the milk, and it was hurting business.

I also wanted to prove to my mother, whom I had felt

failed me in love, that I would be more successful than she was. That the love I had with Ali was tried, tested and true. My mother and I had started speaking again recently, and one thing we could always come together on was the topic of boys. It is why I started writing in the first place. I needed Ali in a way, I needed him so I could feel close with my mom again. My father also always wanted to see me married and with a man who would take care of me. The messages I received from both my parents about my prescribed aspirations in life involved being married and "in love."

My fathers motivations were from a patriarchal standpoint, I should be someone's wife, to be taken care of– off his hands. My mother's motivations probably came from her early middle eastern upbringing, mixed with her own experience with men, love, and sexuality. They both dumped their crap on me and I acted it out in the following drama.

Tuesday, March 2, 2004

> *Hey, how are you?! I'm fine. Well, guess what?! I'm living with my mother again. Yup, we'll see how long this lasts. But we are off to a good start. I feel close, open, and honest around her. I didn't have to move back in, but I did. She didn't have to let me, but she did. Love, Sophia N. Saber*

Wednesday, March 3, 2004

> *Hey, Big cheese! How are you?! Good. You, too? Me, too! So, yah, Alejandro and I talked about hella shit. First off, we met at two, to see the passion of the christ. That didn't work so we walked all over town. No blunts or anything, and we talked about the baby, A LOT. I feel so good. He makes me so happy. He might be the last guy you hear about. I'm not going to say he is the one. I don't believe there is only one. But I love him, and he is who I want. Night Sophia*

Sunday, March 14, 2004

So, it begins… It's 2:29 am …Still waiting for Alejandro. So, he came and got me, took me to go get my shoes. Then we went and got a room for tonight. My last $40. Does he show up? Even call? What would possess me to think he would?! I don't know. So, I'm stuck in this hotel crying again for the second night! And over what?! Alejandro's not my man! But I care about him like he is. I think Montana didn't even do me like this. Alejandro is about to break my heart! I just hope I don't get too hurt. I called the hospital to see if Marisol had gone into labor…Nope. So, I am really curious about his excuse. -Sophia

Tuesday, March 16, 2004

Hey you! The reason he didn't show up was because Marisol was in the hospital with pains. Alejandro was just being a good man and was there for her. I can't be mad at that. I get hurt and cry, but who wouldn't?! I love that man. I guess I'd have to, this is some shit! Well, only four more days till his daughter is born! I am so excited! New life! And she is going to be 1/2 his, so I can love her 1 and 1/2 times more than I normally would! If Alejandro and I do get together I do not want to replace Marisol, I just want to be the baby's friend. To help support her and her father through life, love, and a wonderful new journey! Love Always

Thursday, March 18, 2004

Hey, today has been the worst and best day of my life. I found out that I am pregnant. 3-4 weeks. You know how I found out? I had a miscarriage. I almost had a little boy named Alejandro or a girl. Who knows? I am just glad it was his. I am hurting. I have always wanted a baby. I finally

got one, and BOOM! I lost her right away. Anyway- I told
him, and he was sad. To top it off, we had sex, beautiful
sex. During sex, he says he loves me, and he wants me to
have his baby someday. I know he loves me. I'm telling you,
after today, I know he loves me, and he IS THE ONE!
Love, Sophia

Between my forced and genuine excitement for the birth
of Ali's daughter, and the disappearance of my opportunity
for parenting, I was a ball of rugged, raw, misguided and
devastating emotional highs and lows. I was grasping on to
the fringes of a silver lining in my own catastrophe.

I remember when this happened. I was in a lot of pain,
and the doctors speculated that I miscarried due to elevated
hormone levels and follicles or something— I accepted this di-
agnosis and blew it up into a drama. I needed that attention,
even if it was fleeting, or small, or not all the way truthful.
I needed his eyes focused on me, even if just for a second. I
was trying desperately hard to keep this man's attention, keep
the drama burning, and keep myself from being wrong— es-
pecially when it came time to update my mother. Showing
her I was capable of bearing all that God would put on my
plate was a silent but deadly priority.

Saturday, March 20, 2004

He hasn't ceased to amaze me. Every time I start to doubt
him, or question our love, he lets me know in his way to
stop being afraid, that he is a good man. He really does love
me, and he could take care of me someday, but right now
he has to take care of Marisol and the baby. Anyway, good
night. xoxo Nykol

Monday, March 22, 2004

Welcome, Angelica Marie Gonzalez! Alejandro's daughter was finally born!!! He has a new lady in his life! I had so much doubt. Alejandro is going to change once he sees his daughter. But no- He let me know right away when she was born. I cried. He's a dad and I am not the mother. That makes me sad, but anyway, on an even worse note. My mother kicked me out, because I was wearing pants! Haha! Twenty-two days. Well, I can take care of myself. Happy Miracle of life! <3 Always, Sophia Francine Gonzales Haha! I wish!

Saturday, March 27, 2004

I saw Angelica today! Newborns are not cute. But to me, she is. She looks just like him! Except she is white! Haha. Anyway, Alejandro forgot me again. It hurts so much. I keep putting myself aside for him. And I am hurting myself. That is all. G'night Sophia N. Saber

Wednesday, March 31, 2004

Hey, Diary, I am not OK. My mother is driving me crazy! Everything bothers her! I can't do anything right. I go right, she says go left. I go left, and she complains about how I do it! Anyway, I wanted to tell you about something. The other day, I had an experience with God. I was high, first off. I was talking about Alejandro out loud, to myself, and I was crying, looking at myself in the mirror. Then I realized I was praying. Without even noticing at first. I felt God, and I saw him in me. as crazy as it may sound. I cried, such a stress-relieving cry to God. Everything about Alejandro. He is the only one who knows how badly I have been hurt. I can't help but think this will all be worth it someday. I can't say it enough. I love him. No one said this would be easy. Another woman just had his child. Oh well, it will be my turn someday, right? For now, I am going to concentrate on opening up my own business. The daycare. Getting my GED. Paying my bills & working, hanging out with my bestie. When he is not around, and all of the above have been tended to, and I'm all alone, I spend good quality time with myself. It's given me a lot of genuine thinking time. It's been nice being alone. The 1/2 hour or so that I do see him is all that much more precious. Anyway, I am going to go now. Take a little nappy-poo before work. Love Always, Sophia N. Saber

Thursday, April 1, 2001 Happy April fools day!

Ok, so, here is the new scoop on Alejandro and I. Yesterday, he called me at six to tell me to take a smoke break. I was on my way to clock out so he said to call him. Blah blah blah. I get the same run around from him until noon. He finally calls and picks me up, we drove around Atwater and smoked a blunt. This time was different, he was tired and his mind was not there. Anyway, I don't want to do this. But, I think I might have to let him go... Let him watch his daughter grow up, you know. Love is patient and understanding. Then I can wait for him, because I understand what is going on right now. I have things and he has things. He has work, his daughter, his parents, and friends. I have work, the daycare, my GED. Many things fill my life. We will talk everyday, maybe not see each other. I love him, this is going to work. <3 Sophia N. Saber

Saturday, April 3, 2004

Happy Birthday, Michael. I miss him. Anyway, back to reality! Guess who called me last night?! Marisol! Stupid bitch! She calls me while I am at work. "Sophia, It's me Marisol." Shit! She has me on the spot asking questions about Alejandro! I don't want to lie to her... But...I did. I did it for Alejandro's sake. He called me at about 5 o'clock, talking mad shit about Marisol. About how she complains he doesn't do anything for her! The point is- he called me to tell me about it. He is doing so much for Marisol and Angelica. So much. He is working so hard to provide for his new family! She is so lucky she has him! If I have to let him go for his daughter's sake, bitch better take care of my love! He is my love, my joy, my happiness. Love Always, Sophia N. Saber

Saturday, April 10, 2004

Anyway... So yah, my mom kicked me out again! And for the FINAL time. I had to push my things in a grocery cart to my sister's house! Two trips total! Paris walked with me. It was definitely a humbling experience! That's for damn sure! Anyway, that's all.

Love, Sophia N. Saber xoxo

Sunday, April 11, 2004

Happy, wonderful, joyous Easter!! Hey- just me and you from now on. I want more than anything to be a mother right now. You have no clue! So, Friday Alejandro calls me up and tells me he's trying to get me pregnant. What the hell is that shit?! Is he trying to push buttons or what? He hasn't called for three days... I say it's okay. He'll come around. The truth is...he isn't, he's not going to come. He always surprises me. But Fuck man! I need some love. I need a break! I need some head! I can't ask for those things, I have to find them.

Wednesday, April 14, 2004

Hey, the last couple of days have sucked! I think Alejandro is through with me! I don't know why I can't get him focused. He never calls anymore- I never see him- But I can't. He's never around. I'm getting over him, though. The more he's gone, the less I miss him. I bought a wedding ring today. I don't have his necklace anymore. I gave it back to Marisol on Monday. I went to Alejandro's house. Maybe I'm just making a fool out of myself. Who knows?! Yeah he called after six days! This sucks. Shit fell through as expected. We'll see if I get to see him tomorrow. But, in the meantime, I am sleeping in a public restroom tonight. This sucks ass!! But, this is my mess I got myself into. Nobody else's. I had fun at work tonight. I'm tired. I love you so much! These are hard times. But I will still be breathing tomorrow none-the-less. Good night Love always, Sophia N. Saber

Friday, April 16th, 2004

Hey there! How are you today? I suck. Ali is out. So far. He might come back, but I doubt it. So, I'm kind of bummed out. I need to sleep with him so badly. I took pictures today. They came out nice. There is one in the back for you. But anyway. Officer Brown died today. Or yesterday. Someone shot him. He was Cammie and Isaiah's dad. They came in to workout and brought the kids in all the time. It's so sad. I can't even imagine. Anyway- Later. Love Always, Sophia N. Saber

Saturday, April 17, 2004

Hey you! Crack-head called me at 6:00 am! I have no idea why, but he came and picked me up. We drove around for a while and looked at trailer homes. I am so excited! I want to

*be pregnant soon! He knows it, too. Anyway, I am at work
right now just chillin, watching the cat in the hat. I keep
thinking about Officer Brown. It's devastating. I don't really
want to think about it though. I still don't understand, it's
not part of my thought train, yet. It's sad, I know that much.
Hey, this is my last entry, I guess. So, I love you. You have
helped me through so much by being there for me— oh wait.
I have two pages left. So, bye. Love, Sophia*

Monday, April 19, 2004

*Hey, this for sure is my last entry. So, anyway, I saw
Alejandro Friday. He called me Saturday morning and I
spent all day with him. He didn't drop me off till Sunday
afternoon. As a matter of fact, we had sex all night. It was
nice. Anyway, I talked to my bestie. I told her of my motherhood dreams. She is excited. Well, this is it for sure. Time
to pick up my new Diary. I love you so much! I will visit
you often! Thank you thank you thank you for everything!*

**Alejandro and I had grown into each other for support
as outlets for the reality of the situations we didn't want to
face at home. His self diagnosed entrapment and the inevi-
tability of his inescapable outcome, and my mother issues.
I was homeless and actually living on the streets, sleeping
in out-houses and showering at my sister's place. She didn't
know how bad it was, no one really did. I was still working
and staying clean. Alejandro was an escape for me, he gave
me something to love, a project. Something was broken, and
maybe I could fix it, because fixing myself was proving to be
much more difficult.**

**I was working for my sister full time at her in-home day-
care, spending my days with children and learning from her
how to take care of babies, toddlers and cooking. I spent my
nights sneaking around with someone else's man.**

Sunday, May 2, 2002

Hey, how are you? Me? I'm fine. So, first off, my mom went out of town to Gabriel's in Arizona on Thursday. So, my brother gave me the key to the house and asked me to clean for him. I did. Alejandro and I stayed there Thursday and Friday night. Saturday we got another room. He's been paying a lot of attention to me this last week. It's been nice. I don't want it to go away- but it probably will. Anyway, when we were at my mom's we got drunk and did it on her bed. It was nice, we like, get along so well. I'm laying on his bed right now, spending the night. I didn't want to sleep without him. So tonight's really going to suck. But, yah, regardless. I have a new idea, a new plan. I want to move to Mexico, to Alejandro's grandparents' hometown. To experience life there, you kind of have to survive a little bit more. But my attitude will hopefully get better. It's rotten right now. But yah, I also want to adopt a little boy, Alejandro. That is going to be his name. I told Ali he doesn't seem to care. So, I guess that's a yes. Anyway, happy May Day. By the way, I work for my sister now, so everything should be just fine. Less income, but at least I have one! Well, I'll talk to you later. Love Always, Sophia N. Saber

Wednesday, May 5, 2004

¡Feliz Cinco De Mayo! 20 years ago today, my parents would have been married. Hey! Yesterday, I went on a walk with Ali and his daughter. She is so precious. Although, I feel sort of weird around her. I don't know how to be. I definitely don't want to get attached. I do not like detaching all that much. Alejandro could leave me at any time. I even put him at a safe distance. I don't want my heart to be broken anymore. When he shows me he is serious about me, that I am not just pussy or a good time... then. He told me that

I please him, that I leave him satisfied. I don't really know how to take that. I guess/hope that's a good thing. Ali's really hard to understand. I have to listen to his thoughts and his actions, because his words aren't credible sometimes. Sometimes he just doesn't say things right. I think he has trouble talking, but goddamn that man can listen. I always tease him and say he never listens to me. But the truth of the matter is, he listens so closely he hears what I don't say. He catches my lies too. No one has ever been able to catch my lies, except my father. Now Ali...Love, Sophia

Monday, May 10, 2004

Hey you! How are you doing? Me, just fine. Ok, so, Saturday, I went to work with Ali, and slept in his car until 9am, then I went home. I forgot what happened after that, I guess I went back over there. His dad caught us again. It was nice waking up with him on Saturday. Of course, we smoked. I went home because it was Mother's Day, so I went and saw my mom, and took my brother to the Monster Truck Races. It was so much fun! You have no clue, I wanted Ali to be there, but he had soccer and such. Then we went to a BBQ, which was also fun. Ali and I had a serious conversation. He told me he gets jealous. That's cute. Anyway, he also said that the day his daughter was born, he was thinking about me. I asked him what he could have possibly been thinking about. He said he wondered how it would be to share that experience with me. Then later, he called me crying, saying Marisol had taken the baby out of town with Daniel. That's all for now. Love, Sophia N. Saber

Tuesday, May 11, 2004

Hey, Ali and I had another night last night. That's ok, we haven't had one of those in a while. Hold on...I'm distracted right now...ok, I'm back. Sorry, anyway, he told me 6:00, then 7:00, then 9:00ish. He finally called at 11:00, "Oh- I'm going home, can we please smoke this tomorrow?" "Sure, whatever, yeah." Our relationship is so confusing. We have so many hidden rules, it's not funny. We both know what they are, but we can't talk about the damn rules. BECAUSE THAT'S THE MOST IMPORTANT RULE—-IS THAT YOU CAN'T TALK ABOUT THE RULES OR HOW WE FEEL ABOUT EACH OTHER! It sucks. I just want to tell the world about him, but I can't. I don't think he cares one way or the other. I don't know, everything has been so crazy. My sister's husband's father just died, so she is busy planning the funeral. I am stuck with the daycare all by myself. It's all good, I'm learning, though. Well, I'll be back later. I'm heading out to the store. Love Always, Nyquil

Wednesday, May 12, 2004

Yo! So, Ali and I had a very awkward talk yesterday. You know- he's been saying things like, I satisfy him and I please him, and last night he told me I was like candy!? Yah, I know. We talked about how we both messed up. We should not have gotten close- maybe not. I think I'm going to have to have a talk with him. Maybe we should stop going down this path. I really feel like it's just sex sometimes. I asked him last night. Am I too hard to say no too? He said yes. Yes, I am?! Well then, I will make it easier for him to say no. Man, it's not working point blank. I have to let him go for his sake. FUCK! This sucks! I just lost a good thing. He keeps me sane, he relieves my stress. I hope/pray this isn't it. Sophia N. Saber

Tuesday, May 18, 2004

Hey, so- I left on Friday for Reno, to get my license and see Montana. It was weird seeing him and not being with him. I told him all about Ali. He understood. I told him I loved him, and that was all I needed to say. He didn't even try to hug me or anything. The trip was surprisingly nice. I got to see my dog Sativa. She is getting so big! Anyway, I finally got my license. Frankie picked me up from the bus station and took me to Sandy's. Ali called me, and I went to go see him. Yeah- we had sex for HOURS. The sex was off the hook. It was so long we couldn't even finish, plus we were both blown. But, yah, OMG! He missed me. I could feel it. He said it, but I also felt it. No one makes me feel the way he makes me feel.

Thursday, May 20th, 2004

Hey there, you. I bought a charm bracelet. Well, really it's a watch. So, on my way out of the mall, I stopped at KB to check the price on a toy, and Marisol was there. I didn't even know it! Man, she makes the biggest deal out of nothing! She actually got to me. I really don't know how I feel about some of the things she had to say. She had many valid points, but none of them matter. She said, if he was so into me, how come he never takes me around his friends? How come he never flaunts me? Man, that kind of shit just doesn't matter really. She said his whole family hates me. Even his cousin told her to take flight on me. So she says. But anyway, Ali says that I haven't been acting like myself. I guess I haven't. I don't know what to say for myself. I really don't! Anyway, I was walking home from Ali's and the POLICE pulled me over. I showed them my ID, and they let me go. SNS

I stopped at KB Toys on purpose. I knew she was working, and I wanted to piss her off. Lets keep it real, why I lied like this in my entry is amazing to me. I was so ashamed of my behavior at the time, *and now* I was blatantly lying to myself, my husband, and whoever else asked. It showed in my writing. I guess this is what Ali meant by I haven't been myself. I was changing, becoming a total psycho. The idea of marriage, and all the possessive qualities that come along with it, were eating my soul alive, and I was becoming someone I didn't recognize. Nevertheless, I kept it pushin'.

Tuesday, May 25, 2004

> *HAPPY BIRTHDAY, SISTER! She is 25 years old today. Yeah, anyway, Ali and I slept all weekend at the hotel. We smoked, slept, and fucked. It was the best two days of my life!! That's all for now SNS*

Friday, May 28th, 2004

> *Hey! Yeah, so, Ali and I went to Modesto to do some of his custody papers. So, the battle begins. I paid $430.00 for his attorney. But, anyway, afterwards we went to John's incredible pizza. Angelica is getting big! Love, Sophia*

Thursday, July 9, 2004

> *HAPPY BIRTHDAY, VICTORIA! Hey there, you! It's been a while, huh? Anyway, everything here is all bad once again. I bought a car for $2,500.00. It's a 1992 Ford Explorer, stick shift! Ali and I went on our first road trip to Santa Cruz or Monterey, which was cool. On the 4th, we stopped in Stockton to watch fireworks and went to his friend's house. I'm uncomfortable around his friends. Not to sound like a bitch or anything, but…all of Ali's friends hate*

me. All of his good friends, the ones who know him for who he is, they all say that Marisol is the best thing that ever happened to him. I don't feel like I measure up to her for Ali. She expects everything out of him. I don't. I don't expect anything out of him. And in return, I get nothing. He says he appreciates me, but does he ever mean what he says? He tells me to be patient and things will start to happen. I don't know that I want anything to happen. I am, however, certain I want to have his children. He is going to be a great dad, without question. His mind is truly something spectacular. Ali could never do anything to lose my trust. That sucks, because he does a lot that deserves losing it. But, none of that stuff matters to me. If you love somebody, I don't believe that true love can be broken. It would be like disregarding a family member. You love your son no matter what, even if he/she murders someone. You don't stop loving him/her. I feel that way about Ali. There is nothing that man could do to lose me. Even if we are apart for years. If that is what he wants, let it be. This may sound weird, but I do not want to be his girlfriend. What the fuck is that shit?! This is going to be even more strange, but if we're not married, I can't even do it. He would never marry me for the wrong reasons. So, if he would ever consider marrying me or let alone actually doing it. Yah, I would dedicate the rest of my life to this man. I would be there through it all. I love that boy, he just has no clue! (Now, this isn't going to stalk him or ever beg to be with him) How we are is fine, right now. Of course, we are having our difficulties. I'm going to tell you because I don't tell this shit to anyone. Today, I was going to get him after gymnastics. He tells me I can't pick him up from his house, Marisol is there. No matter what he says, that is his girlfriend! That's his girl. No matter what he or anybody says! I know he cares about me because he lies to me about it. I think it's cute sometimes, but for the most part it just pisses me off. God- I want him to tell me the truth. Wow- I just figured something out...Maybe they are broken up, but just separated, you know...taking a break. Maybe she thinks he is going to come back to her. And, I'll bet you, he is. I know my time with him must be short. I need to enjoy him while he is here. Quit getting mad all the time, sad or hurt. I need to save those emotions for someone who will care about them. I'll explain more later. I'm going to go sit on his face for now. Love, SNS

Sunday, October 3, 2004

Hey, there, you! Such a long time! So, in August– well, August 1ˢᵗ, Ali & I moved into our very first house a year ago this month. For him and me, he's the only guy in my life ever to make it to a year! We have had our moments and fights. It's not how you fight but how long you fight. We're both two second people. I did it! I am opening up my daycare on January 10ᵗʰ, 2005!!

Saturday, October 10, 2004

Hey, I told my father tonight that I wanted to have a baby. He is excited! He and his girlfriend broke up. Like I said, nothing is forever. As For Ali and I, we're doing very well. I think. But I work sometimes, he could just leave me on any day. We got a puppy.

Sunday, November 14, 2004

Hey, you're never going to believe this! Alejandro and I got married.

Thursday, February 17, 2005

*Hey, a lot of time has passed. I hate telling you that, but I have missed more events. My brother, my little brother, you know... He turned 18 on November 6, 2004!!! That's crazy, huh?! On November 9th, Ali and I had the worst fight we had ever had. **And somehow, when it was all over, we found ourselves driving through the snow on our way to Lake Tahoe to elope.** We're way too... how shall I say, dignified to have a Reno wedding. So, off to Tahoe for us. Next, was Thanksgiving. I went to my sister's and ate everything! I went husbandless. I go everywhere husbandless. I hope and pray to God that someday that changes. **Sigh** Married life is ugh... Hard. Ali is high maintenance. I don't even cook for him, I couldn't imagine. Anyway, Christmas is next— he did, however, take me to his company Christmas party. I got him a Sirius satellite radio. We were broke, so I told him not to get me anything. And he didn't. My dad came down from Colorado. He loved Ali! I think! Ali seemed to like him as well. Anyway, on New Years, Ali went out with his buddies, which forced me to go out with mine. I spent most of the night with the kids. Apparently, Ali got too drunk and spent the night sick. Then came my birthday, which was a complete disaster, so I will let Ali tell that story. On January 21st, I got my daycare license! Can you believe it?! I have my own business! I'm only 20 years old! So, the daycare is all set up and running, I have two kids so far. We are running out of money fast, so we got a bank account to start saving, but we can't pay $850 for rent. My husband's proposition is that we move into his parent's house. But I see trouble with that. His sister hates me! But that's ok, I am used to people hating me. I just met his parents a few days ago. What about Marisol? So, what do I do? Let him go?! Live separately for a while? He is talking about buying* *a house with me. DOES HE LOVE ME?!?! He denies me all the time.*

We went to LA, for what I thought was my introduction as his wife. Since that's what I am. He introduced me as his girlfriend, and now he is at his mom's shop, discussing our plans with her. I told him I wanted to talk to his mother about our plans, so that she knows we are serious. But Ali, I dunno, like he wants to keep us separated. I work hard, and for Ali, not for money. I feel like he runs over me. I'm just his stress toy that he wanted in his life forever, that's why he married me. I know he loves me, but his idea of love is a bit different than mine, and that is ok. Cause, so is mine. I mean, I still talk to Montana's mother. I love her. I can call her anytime with any problem and she will be there for me. I want to be a mother like her. See, I did have a good mother role model in my life. You know- this is all my fault, but I never had a celebration geared around me. No graduation, no 19th, or 20th birthday celebrations. No bachelorette party, no wedding, or valentines day. I haven't heard how beautiful I am. I am starting to hate myself. I have had many thoughts of suicide. I feel like God has given me everything I am ever going to have. I still do not have a baby. That's ok. Now is not a good time. Ali and I have to get used to each other first, before we have our Jr. around all the time. There is a lot going on, and I am falling w/o my husband's support. But, I will love him until the day that I die. Love Always, Sophia F. Gonzalez

To this day, I am proud to report I do still love him. Not only because I understand that I am a being made of love and love is what I do as a human, but because he isn't a bad person. We just made some bad decisions together. No love lost. However, the love I was referring to here was not love at all, rather an attachment. A toxic attachment to an idea, a notion society talks about having. If only I knew that I sought love from a man to replace what I had lost or had never been given from my parents, especially my mother; success may have been an option. In any case, I was trying my hardest to achieve unreasonable goals. To remain faithful to promises I could definitely not keep.

My mother came up often in my writing, when I was hurting or mentioning love. Looking back at it now, it was always her I was reaching for, men were just the medium. Missing this love from my own mother began the deep rooted seed of my desire to become a mother. To love my daughter the way my mother never had, so that my daughter might avoid all these words on her pages. Instead, she would seek healthy attachments and joy, and see me as a friend and mentor to support her journey. This was now my new focus. I had begun to give up on ideas of a happy healthy relationship with my mother and started the yearning to be a mother myself. Through continued patterns of toxicity, cause I obviously had not gotten it yet.

Friday, February 18, 2005

> *Good morning! I'm going to get Ali to take marriage classes with me. Basically, we both suck at this. Haha. Anyway- I do not want to live with his parents. I am not looking forward to this! I am still alone. I hope Ali starts to treat me better. I really do, cause I love him so much! My fat guy.*

> *Love Always, Mrs. Gonzalez*

Wednesday, February 23, 2005

> *I feel like I am living someone else's life. Marisol's life to be exact. She was his girlfriend. He promised her forever, not me. But then, he married me. I have never felt so threatened by another woman than I do by her. Because Ali has lost my*

trust, I hate what he has finished doing to me and what they started. I know he loves me, just like he loved Marisol just like I'm sure he would never cheat on her, I'm still in question as to why he married me?! Ali always has hidden agendas, our communication skills suck. I'm confused I thought your wife was supposed to be everything to you?! I screwed myself. I knew the situation, but Marisol came first, not me. How do I push her aside and not angelica? Hopefully they figure it all out. Him and T are supposed to talk today. haha. whatever SNS

Friday, February something, 2005

Hey, there! I got a daycare call today! For two kids. I am almost 1/2 way there! Anyway, Ali and I, you know... here is all I could come up with. When we married each other neither of us really knew what to do. It might take some time- he will get to where he needs to be, as will I. Until then, I have to put up with his shit and he has to put up with mine. If I want the end result, I have to face what is now. I love him. I know I am for him, and he is for me. Love, Mrs. Gonzalez

Wednesday, March 2, 2005

Hey, there. My Husband hates me. Yesterday, not the day before yesterday, we were tiffing. I gave Devon a ride home. Ali was all pissed about it. So, he went to sleep without a kiss or anything, he wouldn't even admit he had a problem until 4:00 am! All he said then was, "You should not have given that man a ride home. He has plenty of friends." Whatever. You should not have gone to Marisol's house for three hours, or at all!!! Now, we're even, bitch! Ohhh, he makes me so angry! I can not keep up with him! It feels like a new deal every day! Which it is. He called me just *now from work, basically to tell me I have to shut down the daycare, and re-open when we move into his parent's house. I am absolutely pissed and not happy at all! I am out of work for three months while we live with his parents. He says I don't have to work, I can just watch the two little ones. We'll spend the money I make and save the money he makes. I hope all of this works out and he doesn't give up. He might hate me now, but he will love me forever. I know he will. Love, Mrs. Gonzalez*

Tuesday, March 3, 2005

It seems like I only write to you when I have something mean to say about Alejandro. I can't say that to him. He gets mad at me for getting mad at him. This time, he is mad at me first. I want to get mad back, but I can't. He'll leave me. Shhhh, I am not supposed to know that, I guess. Montana called, drunk, apparently, saying I called him. I did, but not to talk. I was returning a missed call from a random Reno number. Anyway, Ali says I have no business talking to him. So, I guess this means he has no business talking to Marisol? Let's go back one week. Ali went to Marisol's house for three hours! To do what?! Talk about Angelica?! I don't think so! But he is mad at me?! So mad, in fact, he doesn't want me around his daughter. But he loves me?! I hate this unsure feeling of not knowing what is going to happen next! I feel like he would just leave me at any given time, for any reason. He has never really tried to keep me, not the way he can't let Marisol go. I understand he still has to get over her. I have to give him time, but how much?! I am realizing that Marisol and Montana aren't so different. Marisol still loves Ali the way Montana still loves me. And they always will. Ali touched Marisol in a place in her heart that she'll never forget. I touched Montana's heart, but neither Marisol nor Montana could touch our hearts the way we touch each other's hearts. Yes, there is still love for the ex's, but not the love Ali and I have. He is my husband, and I am his wife. No other man or woman will get in my way. They might cause us bad days, but they will not ruin my marriage. I only hope my husband feels the same way. He doesn't seem to get it, but I have all the time in the world for that man. He and I have a shit load of learning to do. It will hurt both of us, but in the end~ the man doesn't even trust me with Angelica! What can I do to make him understand?! "God?!" -SNS…this is me

Sunday, March 14, 2005

Hey, you will never believe where I am. Texas. With my Uncle J and Aunt P. And my mother. She just had a hyster-ectomy, so she is being a pain in my ass, as usual. Yeah, I am with my family. It feels so weird, but I love it. J and I talked for about 4 hours the night we got there. He is SO different from my mother! Anyway, I got a lot out, and he wanted to hear about it. He cares about me, I think?! I asked a lot of marriage questions, and he gave me some sound advice. I am going to keep in touch from now on! He is my family and my only uncle! Not technically, but as far as blood family, he's it. Our whole family situation sucks! He feels the same way. Alejandro is at home. I wonder if he misses me or my pussy?! I hope it's me. I love him, I love him, I love him. He does something for me, I dunno, I miss the shit out of him. On Thursday, we had Angelica. Well, I had Angelica, he was tired. It's ok, I am starting to get comfortable around her! Her little face brings so much joy to me! When she smiles, I feel warm. I think she and I are going to be close. I hope. She walked around the block three times with Sandy's kid and I. I love these two so much! My nieces are getting big and learning so much, so fast! Life is confusing, and I want my husband. Love Always, Sophia N. Gonzalez

Monday, March 14, 2005

*Good evening. I figured it out. He hates me. He does.
Slowly but surely, Ali is realizing he doesn't like me so
much. If that's not it- he is pregnant. Everything I do bothers
him! Everything! I wish he loved me the way he did. I know
I have changed, but I thought he loved me no matter what?! I
think something is terribly wrong. I think he regrets marrying
me. It scares me because we are moving in with his mom and
the whole family. I cannot communicate well or even at all.
This is going to frustrate me at times. Ali sucks at the inter-
pretation thing. I constantly have to talk to him. "What?"
"Huh?" What did she say? You know? But only when I
hear my name or a title that applies to me. I am so scared!
OMG. Ali doesn't respect me 1/2 as much as he should!
If he doesn't respect me, his family won't either! He puts on
a good face, but when it is just him and me alone, we are
at each other's throats non-stop! I wonder why he hates me.
What did I do? You know, my mother gave me some sound
advice this weekend. She said that affairs start when one
feels incompetent. If I keep him happy, he won't cheat. But,
obviously, he is not happy. What more can I do for him? Or
what should I stop doing? He is lying in the bed next to me
with his back turned. I will never give him a card or a letter!
He hates me! Jesus- Please help me help my husband help
me be a better wife for him. Love, Mrs. Gonzalez*

Friday, March 18, 2005

*There's family drama! =) But it's my family drama! My
mother is mad at me for talking bad about her. Oh, well, my
uncle J is trying to help me deal with her. I am so glad for
him. I guess my grandmother and aunt are coming out here.
We'll see what happens. Anyway, Ali had his daughter's
baptism class tonight. Things are going well with Ali and his*

parents. The daycare is all set up and ready to be used. I hope Ali and I start finding some common ground. Seems like we are. Just like everything, I have to give it time. Famous words from my husband. Love, Mrs. Gonzalez

Wednesday, May 18, 2005

Well, the drama I never finished writing~ Angelica's birthday party. I was cool. I acted like she wasn't bothering me (Marisol). She really wasn't. Next was Angelica's baptism. My supposed husband didn't even invite me! It hurt me so bad! I know he and Marisol still have something! Well, it's May 18th, guess what I just found out this past weekend?! Ali cheated on me. Wait- it gets better. She is pregnant. and guess who?! Marisol. This is like a goddamn Twilight Zone episode! Again? Ali says he wants me to stay. I think he can't afford for me to leave. I know he wants Marisol. I want him to have his woman, excuse me, 'girl,' too. I gave so much of myself to him. I feel sorry for the next man that tries to love me. I can't say I will never love again. I love being in love. I loved being involved with Ali. I would have been faithful to him for the rest of my long-lived life. I made a promise to him and before God to stay faithful. But here is the tricky part- I also promised to stay by my man, through thick and thin, for better or for worse. Since he broke his promise, does that mean it is the end of our life together? I want to stay. I love him so much. I made the wrong decision the first time, and I can't do it to myself again. How could I be so fucked up to myself?! So many times in a row! First, Michael, then Montana, now Ali! Those first two are forgiven, I don't think I will ever forgive Ali. He had no choice with Marisol; he knocked that bitch up. He chose me. He married me! He doesn't want me. He wants Marisol! I asked him why he did it?! He said he needed reassurance. That mother-fucker (literally). You do that before you say, "I do." He ruined my

life. Now, I am going to ruin his. Just give me a year. love
me. only you know me.

Reading these words now, I not only acknowledge what
an adult situation this was to be handling at such a young
age, but how patented these notions were. I was so perplexed
because I was following a predetermined path shoved down
my cis–gendered throat since I was born. I was supposed to
aspire to marriage and have the drama. The things that go
along with following someone else's path, or following the
path you think will bring you closer to your mother.

I didn't have my intuition guiding me yet. I was still led
by what I thought was expected of me, without any direct
influence from either of my parents. Societal indoctrination
is a more powerful influencer, then and now. Especially now.
Religious notions drove the girl in these pages. Notions from
a place where she had once found love. It just so happened
that she was applying the lessons in all the wrong ways.

Wednesday, May 18, 2005

> *I'm confused, I'm confused, I'm SO confused! I don't know*
> *what to write about! I'm so confused. I thought Ali was*
> *somebody else. He is not who I thought he was. Nobody can*
> *help me. Lord knows I need help right now! I wish someone*
> *could make up my mind for me. If I stay with him, I am*
> *going to make him miserable. I don't particularly want to do*
> *that. We have suffered enough. I cannot believe he is doing*
> *this to me. Yeah, he cheated. Yeah, the bitch is pregnant.*
> *But he lied to me. He admitted that he was never going to*
> *tell me about it if she wasn't pregnant. That's why I want*
> *to leave him. He is a liar, and he is good at it. But here is*
> *why I am confused. His actions are telling me he does not*
> *want to be with me. But his words say that he does. So who*
> *or what do I believe. I need somebody to listen to his side of*

the story and tell me the truth about him. A professional. But who? Where? When? How? What do I do if Ali does not cooperate? Do I leave? Does that mean he can't tell me he doesn't want to be with me? Why is he with me? Why did he marry me? This isn't good, if I am still questioning our marriage maybe it's time to leave. My dad said this... "The first time, you missed all the red flags. So, God had to turn up the volume so you could see what kind of a man Ali is." That's so true. I think my father is correct. Either way, I don't feel like I can just up and leave him. I have to stay and see if we can just work this out. I doubt it. Ali doesn't seem like he wants to. It's basically up to him.

I love you, Sophia Nahlah Saber, if you are still in there. I am sorry for doing this to you, changing your name, giving your body to a man who doesn't seem to love you 1/2 as much as he should. I am sorry for allowing you to trust another man so much. Next time, I will listen to you, I promise. If I leave him, I will date again. Maybe not very soon, but I will. In a way, I am grateful to Ali- the way I am grateful to Montana. He put his hands on me. He did it before me and will continue after me. Ali cheated before, WITH me, and he will continue after me. Hold on. I have to get my niece some chocolate milk...ok back. Ok, I won't lie- I think it would be so wonderful to be single again. Stress-free! But in the long run, I want to be married. To whom? Well, I thought Ali was going to be my forever. Turns out, he is not. I don't get it. Why is he with me if he wants to be with her so bad? At first, I felt bad for Marisol. In a way, I respected her. She lost the man she loved and was left with her daughter. Then she fucked my husband. Now, she is pregnant with a married man's child. So, should I stay?! Make them both suffer, including myself? Or should I just go and free all three of us? I wish someone could tell me the truth. Love me, please love me. In Jesus name.

My editor wants my current thoughts here. All I can think is, damn, it's been 20 years, and I'm still telling myself the same exact thing.

Saturday, June 11, 2005

> *Hey, there. Some days are good, and some days are bad. Today, I think, is going to be bad! It's almost been four weeks since I found out, and I am still convinced Ali wants to be with Marisol. I don't know why I stay with him. Yeah- I love him. I want to love myself more! I miss me... So much! I used to be funny and light. Now, I am serious and hard. Hard to make smile. My health is still horrible. I never eat. I hope I die by the time I am 30. I am ready to die now, but I could never take my own life. That is for God to take. I find myself alone and sad most days. I try not to let Ali see it. He gets mad. I still cry to sleep. I am so unhappy- yet I can't leave him?! He broke his promise to me, point blank. I should have gotten it, but I didn't. God be with me in these dark and perilous times. Love, Mrs. Gonzalez*

Monday, June 13, 2005

> *My father is angry with me, I can hear it in his voice when I call. He says. "Sophia, what do you need? I am kind of busy." He is angry with me for staying with Ali. I bet if I said I left Ali, he'd drop what he was doing to listen, w/o me having to ask. One thing about my dad, no matter how mad at me he gets, if I tell him I need to talk, he always listens. I get it. I miss him a little more every day. My little brother, too. He's a pot-head now, that sucks, I did it, it's my fault! I don't feel the need to try and stop it, though. He has a girlfriend named Kathy. I like this girlfriend the most because I hear the least about her. He seems to like her the most, too. Night.*

Tuesday, June 14, 2005

Hey, I give up. That is all. I give up. I am done. I have tried everything now, so that is all.

Sunday, June 16, 2005

It's dark. I can't see the lines very well. I miss my dog, Sativa. I have fallen in love with Mr. Gonzalez, again. Love, Mrs. Gonzalez

Friday, June 17, 2005

I lost my daycare, Sativa, my husband, and my mind. I feel crazy. Yes, it is a problem! I told Ali of my sexual fantasies. He didn't judge me, or even get weirded out. He fulfilled them. I only told him 1/2 or maybe 1/3, but he fulfilled what I told him. I'm confused- I don't know if I will make it in this life. How come we never travel anymore? He tickled me last night and made me laugh. Sex is still something amazing. How come I only feel beautiful in bed? Ali's cousin is coming into town today. I like him. He favors me in my thoughts. I don't know what track my train is on. Maybe I got derailed somewhere along the way. He should be here around 2:00 or 3:00. Ali left to drink with his uncle after work. We will see how that goes. Bertha, Ali's sister— we have been hanging closer, kind of. I feel she is faking it with me. Everything here is so weird to me. She is a girl. We all know how that goes. Ali and I have to move out of here. We are newlyweds. We are supposed to be finding our groove. Instead, his parents are trying to put us in their little groove. I don't want to be his Mexican wife. I just want to be his wife. The one he married, not the one they want me to be. When I have kids, I will start cooking. Until then, Ali is a grown-ass man. I'll have to learn Spanish to communicate with my in-laws. I guess we'll go back to school to get our GEDs. Then off to college. Ali has a plan. He wants to work in a prison or be a probation officer. He wants me to work. Truth be told, I just want to be a housewife. Love, Mrs. Gonzalez

Sunday, June 19ᵗʰ, 2005

Happy Fathers Day! I miss my dad so much. If I wasn't still married, I'd move back in with my dad, once again, proving that life can be however you make it. Ali and me, ugh- I am so tired of arguing with him. I guess on Friday night, some people at a party were making fun of him for not buying me a nicer ring. But he knows, like I know, I don't want a nice ring.

Monday, June 20, 2005

Hey, Ali is at his mediation thing with Marisol. I didn't go because he didn't want me there. I don't think Ali wants a marriage with me. I forgot to get him something for Father's Day. Marisol didn't forget, though. I don't belong here. It's hard to say I don't belong to Ali because I don't believe it. All he is doing is hurting me. The longer we're together, the more we fight. His family hates me. It's becoming very apparent that nobody wants me here. Not even my husband. He is out with his other life. Why can't I leave him, damnit?! Our relationship has hit rock bottom. We need help. He's not willing. If I leave him, I will get a divorce. I'd move to LA, eventually. I'd miss him, but one or three months after my departure, Marisol and Ali will find each other once again. People say that Ali and I are good together, and good for each other. I used to see it. I used to believe it. Now, all I see are lies, cheating, and deception. Malicious acts, and unkind words. I am dying inside again. The only solution I

*see to this problem is to have my own secret life. Maybe cheat
on him. And I would never tell him, unless I got pregnant.
Why not? These are the games he plays with me. I need to
start keeping myself happy. Because nobody in this world can
love me the way I love me. Or maybe it's just time for me
to go? Just leave him. I just have to wait for him to realize
a divorce would be best. I don't want this to be one-sided.
Love, Sophia F. Gonzalez*

Same Day, Four Hours Later

*It's 7:39 pm. Last I heard from Ali, it was 4:00, and he
was going to be back around 5:00 ish. I wonder what his
excuse is this time? Anything but the truth. I have no clue
where he is at, not even a clue. All I know is that he is not
where he said he would be. I want him to let me go. He does
not need me here. He really doesn't. I have to think about
the rest of my life… To be a step-mom & a bad wife. To
always come second? No. It's not, and the longer I am here
depressed and unhappy, the more depressed and unhappy I
am making my husband. I am falling apart. I haven't the
slightest clue on how to fix myself. He's home. It:s 7:47.
Let's hear his excuse…later*

Tuesday, June 21, 2005

*Here I am, at his job, and I haven't the balls to tell him I
am leaving him. I just told him what his dad said. What a
fucking mess. His excuse yesterday…"I just got out."*

Thursday, June 23, 2005

*He didn't give it back. I will never get my husband back.
What can I do? Ignore him, too? He won't let me move out.
So, I don't know. I think we are bankrupt. Well, maybe just*

a dollar. I can only see us having a future together if I turn my head and expect absolutely nothing out of him. I want to help him make me happy, but he doesn't want me to have that. He wants happiness for himself. I have always said, nobody can love me the way I love me. I thought he could. I thought Ali loved me just as much as i love myself. But he, like me, only loves himself. I loved Ali as much as he loved himself. I do! I need to back off of him for a while. I'll quit caring so much about him. I'll just let him do whatever he wants. I have meant to do this, but I haven't had anything to do while not stressing about him. I wish I would hurry up and get pregnant. I could leave and then take a nine-month vacation in sunny Colorado. I can't tell Ali what to do with his life. I see that now. I know he gets this pussy, forever, I see it. It's the only time we're not arguing. Fucking sad, isn't it?! I'm so tired. Thank you for letting me bitch. Love, Sadly Mrs. Gonzalez

Friday, June 24, 2005

Hey, I just watched my heart beating. It was royal. My stomach spits up about 1/2 of everything I eat. I have IBS. Stands for Irritable Bowel Syndrome. I feel better now that I know what is wrong with me. It feels good to take care of myself. I woke up early this morning and cleaned the house for a bit. I sat and cried for a while. Hey- I am still healing. Besides, I can cry as long and as often as I want. The doctor is going to put me on some anti-depressant. I can't wait- I think I'm ready. I need to be in control of myself. It's what he wants and needs, but more importantly, I want and need it. I want my confidence back- I want to feel beautiful again. I know he can't do it. I can, though. I am done relying on Ali to make me happy, for now anyway~ he might get it someday?! I hope I still love him. I know he loves me. I need to help him learn to not be so selfish. He is very selfish. Not by choice. By birth. I believe we are all born with certain traits. Mine were beauty and wisdom. Neither is developed, but that is why life is so long. Bottom line, I married an ASSHOLE! What of it, I guess? Anyway, I knew life here wouldn't work, I'm too lazy, and my attitude (apparently) sucks. Ali has asked me to make some changes lately. My attitude and something else, but it was so preposterous of him to ask me to change who I am. And he thinks we are almost bankrupt! Ali is not my life, he is one part of it, like a chapter in a book. He consumes me and hurts me almost daily, but I don't want to care. It hurts too much to care about Ali. I love him, I do, but he treats me like dog shit. I hope he will get it and love me how I deserve to be loved. I know he has it in him. Love, Me

June 25, 2005

How cute! My mother called me for advice. I wanted to hang up on her, but she started yelling at me. "Sophia! I called you because I was feeling guilty about the money! I need you! Am I wrong?! Tell me, what do you think?! I may have done a lot wrong in my life, but if your mother calls you for advice, you have done something right. Love, me

Thursday, June 30, 2005

Man. I hate everything. Myself, my place of residence, my husband. I am dark right now. I have been swimming every day since Monday. Today, Paris came out and swam with me for about half an hour. He asked me if I thought he and I would have been happy together. He says I never gave him a chance. It's true, I didn't. I married Ali instead, cheating, lying bastard! I could have any guy. Paris is out of the question now. Ali was the only one I was willing to go through this with. The only one. Life's a bitch. Love, Me

Friday, July 1, 2005

Happy July 1ˢᵗ. I have been on an antidepressant for five days now. I feel just as bad as I did five days ago.

Monday, July 4ᵗʰ, 2005

HAPPY HAPPY FOURTH OF JULY! My favorite holiday. I love fireworks. I don't quite understand the politics, but I will.

Wednesday, July 6, 2005

Hey, how are you doing? Me? Well, I have something to tell you, something new that is. I keep reading parts of you to Ali. I don't know why, I just do. I have trouble putting thoughts in my head into words. Give me some paper and a pen and I can write my thoughts down as they come to me. Well, right now, I have to go. My husband is starting to bug me. He is impatient, so I am going to stop writing for now. He keeps writing to you, sorry! He needs to do it right this minute, he is humping me! Say hi, Ali-"hola." See what I mean?! Anyway, it's been a week on my anti-depressants, and there are still no noticeable changes. Love, Mrs. Gonzalez

Thursday, July 7, 2005

Dear Alejandro,

Love, how was your day? I guess you want to know where I am at?! Well, probably my sister's. Anyway, I am scared. I don't know if I can raise your two children. I don't know how this happened, but I am holding on to you by a thread. How do I feel? I am scared. Deathly scared. Do you think I can do it? Help me, if you think I can. Help me find strength. Every day that goes by, I feel a little more dead. I miss you. I miss me! I miss us! It feels weird writing to you in my diary because, well, it's my diary, not stationary. Anyway, about this weekend. I don't feel right. Your mother doesn't have anything nice to say about me. So, how much of a chance do I stand?! I am scared and nervous! I am losing my mind! I had a dream that I adopted a little boy last night, and some lady was trying to kill us because she wanted him. That's all. Love always, Sophia

Tuesday, July 12, 2005

Hey, let me show you something. My life with Ali: step-mother to two children, one conceived during our marriage, always coming second, his whole family hating me and wishing I was Marisol, having to stay in Merced, and becoming a housewife. My life without Ali: well, no Ali. I would be alone, with more room to grow. I want to be recognized for the wonderful woman I am, and can be. I gave Ali so much of me. I treated him so well, and he still cheated on me. Ali should be with Marisol. I think she is good for him. He loves her. She is his number one, and the mother of his children. Also, if I stay, I could never have his children. I have always wanted to be a mother, not a stepmother. I keep saying I need to decide, stay or go. I already made a choice. To stay. But not have his kids? That's not fair to me. He still gets me. For as long as I am with Ali, I will be unhappy. I let him in, and now he has ruined me for me. I am stuck with two kids that aren't mine. He hid me for so long because he knew what he was doing was wrong. So, why does he continue?! I guess this is why they say you should wait to get married. I won't be happy until Ali and I are divorced. How do I start to leave him?! I missed my period this month, but I bled hard for one day. Love, Me

Thursday, September 9, 2005

> *Hey, sorry I haven't had time to write to you. I have been
> stressed out lately. Hopefully, this is the worst my life will
> ever be. Ali is having a son.*

Monday, September 12, 2005

> *Hey, you. I haven't been writing to you because I don't
> know what to say. A lot has been going on. I just don't quite
> know how to put my feelings on paper. I don't know what I
> am feeling. I might be married, I might be divorced. I won't
> even know until Marisol has the baby. Even then, just what
> if? Anyway, I am going to go now. I am afraid of myself.
> I have never, in my life, been so out of touch with myself. I
> am trying to improve, I am trying to save my marriage. It's
> the only one I ever want to have.*

Wednesday, October 5, 2005

> *It's been almost three months, and our car window is still
> broken. A lot has happened, I guess. I am still with my
> decision to stay with Ali. I married him. As much as I am
> not ready for Ali to have another baby, I am not prepared to
> get a divorce. What if I am supposed to be married to this
> fool? Love, Sophia N. Saber*

Wednesday, October 5, 2005

> *Hey, there, you. Again. So, anyway, every day since we
> first moved into our new place, I have been cooking. Every
> night, I have been practicing my wife skills. I was doing
> his laundry every weekend, having his lunch packed every
> night. I even try to give him head spontaneously to keep
> him interested. But it all feels like, no matter what I do for*

him— even loving his daughter with the same unconditional and fiery intensity that I love him with— it will never be the same as if I had his son or daughter. Now, I never will. How do I do for my husband what another woman has done and continues to do? How is this supposed to work? It just has to. I am the one who couldn't wait to get married. I had to say yes to his proposal, right? Anyway, I am almost off- talk to you later. Sophia

Thursday, October 6, 2005

I want to tell him right now that it is over. But whenever I try to talk to him, he shuts me up. We haven't had sex in six days. I wonder if he's leaving home again. I doubt it, but maybe. I feel like he is waiting for me to leave him. I am waiting for him to leave me! Shit! He says he wants to be married, but we all know what that means. What a fool I've been, what a fool. Now, all there is to do is wait. We're at a point where we both want each other to change. But changing someone is none of your business unless your name is God. Ali is who he is, no matter if I like it. Shit, no matter if anyone likes it, Ali is who he is. Forever stuck in his ways. How did we get here? I never wanted to change my Ali- he used to listen to me so well! I guess I didn't sound like a broken record then. He wants me to change, as well. I know that being a good wife for Ali will never be enough for him. He sleeps, eats, smokes, and watches TV all day. He doesn't even need me. Sophia, who I am, he doesn't need anymore. I am just a sex object. I'm sure when he looks at me at night, he just wants to get it in. He hasn't tried to please me in like three months. I quit, too. I'm hurting from him, though. How come he is the one crying? The finances, maybe? Maybe he is holding on for finances sake? Just do it, Sophia. Just go out there and fucking tell him you're leaving!

October 7, 2005

Ali's mom invited me to a family wedding. It dawned on me that Marisol would be present. Normally, I wouldn't mind. However, she is nine months pregnant with my husband's son. I am in no mood to lay eyes on that. This is starting to go on too long. I am completely alone. Love, Sophia N. Saber

Monday, October 10, 2005

Hey, today is the day... I will go to get annulment papers. I give up. Today. I give up. I gave him a year, and in that time, I have hurt and cried more than I have my entire life. I hate to do this. More than anyone, I love him. I truly do. This isn't about him cheating on me, this is about how he is now treating me. At this point, I have realized no matter how many talks we have or how he says he loves me or wants to be with me, it will never work. I went to the wedding Saturday night. We had a great time. His family pulled together and faked some smiles for me, so I pulled together and faked some smiles for them. I ended up getting drunk. The night before, I had asked to go out with my sister. He said no, I had to watch Angie. Well, after we got back from the wedding, all I wanted to do was ride, but he called his friends and went out to the bar till 3:00 am. I don't care anymore. He can do whatever he wants. Marisol now lives with his parents. This will never get any better. It will only get worse and in my favor. I need to leave him before we have to divorce. That way it can be annulled. I mean, c'mon! We got married in SWEAT PANTS after a fight! Of course, this is how it ends. Of course. -SNS

Tuesday, October 11, 2005

Hey! I did it! I told him I wanted to be separated. I didn't want to say divorce. Anyway, it was sad and pathetic. Nothing I said got through to him. I know that being nice is unusual for me, but in this instance, I was trying my hardest to be nice. But he cut me off so quickly, almost immediately. He hated me. He said at that moment, I broke his heart. I never meant to hurt him, never. I know this is going to hurt and take some time, but it has to be done, before we start hating each other more. He can no longer keep me happy, and has expressed to me that I no longer make him happy. He needs me to change, but he doesn't know how. This may be the end of our marriage, but I hope it's not the end of us. I have to let him go. If he truly loves me, he will return. Truth is, I know he won't. He loves himself way too much. I don't know what I am going to do without him. It was so hard to do what I did yesterday. After all was said and done, we made love. It felt so good. But we still need to separate. Sex can no longer decide my fate. No matter how good it is. It is just sex. Love Lastly, Sophia N. Gonzalez

Wednesday, October 12, 2005

Hey there you, How are you? I'm fine. I guess we're back at square one. Because I can't leave him! I just can't believe that something is holding me to him. I don't know what. Marisol is all big and pregnant. I guess you could say that he is on probation. Tomorrow I am going to talk to a lawyer just in case his ass has lied to me again. He knows what he has done and now he knows how to fix it. If he does it I will be more than willing to take him back and stay. But he needs to cut his shit out. Love, Sophia

Wednesday October 19, 2005

> *Hey there, you. Ali and I have had our last fight. Everything was fine yesterday. I swear. Angie and I came home to him together and gave him big kisses. I was supposed to leave to get some pizzas for my sister, the girls, and us. I jumped in the shower after him, because I stunk pretty badly. When I got out, Angie was sitting on the couch alone, and my truck was gone! I was pissed!! Ali eventually came back with the pizza, and I was even more upset! He demolished my whole plan! I blew up at him, and he blew up back! We immediately took Angie home because we were fighting so much. We destroyed the house, pulled down our curtains, and punched up the bedroom door.*

Monday, October 24, 2005

> *"When I close my eyes and begin to pray, I think I see a way that you and I could stay." Hey there, you! I took Angie to church with me yesterday. It was nice. Michael kept looking back at me. After the sermon, he came up to me and said, "Sophia, the older you get, the more beautiful you get." I said thank you and walked away. I wanted to punch him in his freaking face! I hope, over time as he sees me, he regrets that one Thursday! I could have just loved him! I've never found myself since him. I know I've gone through all this to grow, despite him. I would be a mother. I know what I heard God say -SNS*

Thursday, November 3, 2005

> *Hey, you'll never guess where I am right now. The hospital. My step-son is being born. I think it could be a girl or not his at all. It could come out Black or Chinese or something. I'm in a surprisingly good mood. Should I be? I'm so nervous,*

my teeth are shaking so bad, I have to bite on my lips. I only have one cigarette left, and I had better save it. Ali is going to want some. On our way over here, I told him to be nice to Marisol today. Not, I wanna fuck you when this is over 'nice,' but you are the biological mother of my children, and I have love for you' nice.' Two different messages. He already went into the place that I am not allowed to and hasn't come out for quite some time. So I left. Went outside to smoke my cigarette. The pain is fading the more I write. I'm in this garden. Hold on, I need to check the sign. "Designated smoking area." But it's a square garden surrounded by glass windows to sick people's rooms? I'm super uncomfortable smoking out here. I hope Ali finds me. All he has to do is look out the window. Besides, I told him as soon as he disappears, I will too. Here I am. Nowhere. What on earth am I doing this to myself for? I would be so much happier without him. But something is holding us together, through this God-awfulness Anyway- what if this is my meaning? What if there is such a thing as destiny, fate, or even God? Then, for all of those reasons, I must remain faithful. I knew from a young age that the people closest to me would be the ones to hurt me the most. Starting with my mother, who to this day, rebukes me. Well, it finally happened. Ali Jr. was born at 8:27 am, weighing in at 7 lbs. 13 oz. I got to see him and take a picture with him. There was no drama whatsoever. Ali and I pulled it together today. We welcomed our son into this world together. This is our son. Ali is upset that the boy is not mine. But he is. These are our kids. This is our life, our family. Ali Jr. has some of Ali's markings, so I know he is Ali's. Well, Sophia. He is his, and he is a boy. Now what?!? SNS

Thursday, November 17, 2005

There is this pain that I have been hiding, and the longer I hide it, the more I change to accept the way you are. But now, I have run out of places to hide my pain and anger. I'll never really be happy until I am free from me. I need to stop writing now and leave. When I return home, my husband will be gone, and the emptiness will soon set in. Life will begin to fade. I can no longer wait. It's new. We just began. Words we say over time. We are getting no younger. Instead of feeling empowered and delivered by my husband, I felt killed and ran over. I will always love you, Alejandro. You are my husband. When I return, my home will be empty, and you will be gone. My marriage is over, and I am to blame. Lesson learned.

CHAPTER 7

MC

Noun: *The Initials she wanted me to use for her name.*

Ali and I had separated. I moved in with my best friend and her toddler son. They lived in a small two-bedroom apartment on the other side of town. It was a transitional period that would allow me extra room to explore my other interests. Things I should have explored as a kid in a safe environment. However, that's not my story. This is when that part begins, in the wild, operating in disguise, pretending to be an adult. I was interested in my body, my emotions, and music.

Sam and Mariah, who fill the next chapter, were working on becoming part of the industry. I felt safer exploring what was occurring with Sam. He met most requirements that I needed to report back home, including being a man. It satisfied the heteronormative expectations I had internalized from my parents and from the church shoving them down my throat.

It probably wouldn't have crossed my mothers mind that I might be interested in a woman. The truth is that I was. I was more interested in what I was feeling with Mariah, but was terrified to write about it. I was even more terrified to express the relationship sexually. I was probably a bit scared from the incident at Daniel's house when I was 15. With the very real threat of the male gaze disrupting my sexual exploration, I was closed off to the idea subconsciously. But I

was in exploration mode, and I couldn't ignore the nagging feeling in my heart that was drawing me closer to her.

Friday, February 24, 2006

> *Hey, I haven't been writing because life has gotten busy for me. The divorce from Ali, the falling out over my rebound, Sam, the confusion of sexual preference, the surfacing of deep rooted anger. I am starting to have some real strange and strong symptoms. Like, I think I might be gay. It's something I have always thought about, but never really acted upon. I mean, I was raised in the church, and it's wrong in the Lord's eyes, right? Then why do I get butterflies when she calls? Why do I see me with her? Why can I feel myself able to love her? She is a SHE. It's a new thing. It's like being young, and having my first crush. I don't know what I want or like in a woman, or if I even actually like girls. Am I just hurt? I have been talking to Mariah for exactly a week. Ali and I have spoken for the last time... about eight times this week. I finally went and got the papers. I am so done with this bullshit. Sam called to tell me pictures from the wedding we went to together were done. Fuck! I want him so bad! I know I'll never have him. I'm excited about my feelings toward Mariah and what they could mean.*

Monday, March 13, 2006

> *Sam got a hold of me about two weeks ago. He needed some back up vocals for a track. It came out good. Turns out he does like me. And to think, this whole time, I thought he didn't. He says he just wants to take things slow. He was in a five year relationship with his ex. He says he is fucked up from that. I guess she just toyed with his heart. Even though we already slept together, we won't again until we are sure about one another. He is smart and careful with his heart.*

He doesn't act like he's all booty in love with me. I thought he was too good for someone like me. Guess I might be worth something after all. Anyway, on Friday, we took his kids roller skating. It was soooooooo much fun! On Saturday, we took them to Monterey Bay Aquarium. My sister and the girls came with us. We didn't act like a couple, it was nice. I really enjoy his kids. Apparently, they enjoy me too. They never want me to leave! Haha. His brother, whose name is also Alejandro (funny, huh?), and his wife, Lainy, likes me too. It's so nice to be liked! He doesn't have a shit load of family, just enough. They are all hella cool. Saturday night, we lay awake all night sharing our deepest secrets with one another. It was romantic. We mostly talked about our exes, and what we want from life, till the sun came up. No sex. He says I am beautiful when I sleep. Love, Miss Saber

With Sam, I was clearly running from something. Not just the end of my marriage, but feelings for a woman I had just met. I had not yet wanted to face the facts about what I was feeling inside. I was still outwardly Christian, and wanted to keep up appearances for the sake of my mother. Around this time, if our conversations were not about boy drama, they were about my return to God. I was always thinking about my mother in relation to my relationships, including the one I had with God.

It was far more acceptable for my mother (under the influence of religious and heteronormative dogma), to accept a poor or abusive heterosexual relationship, one where complacency was the norm, than it was to accept a homosexual relationship. Sam was who I could talk to my mother about. Maybe I would bring him to church and save his soul. Mariah was who I wanted to explore heaven with. But it always felt like we were a little bit dirty.

April 8, 2006

Hey there, you! I have to drop off Sam's stuff to him today. I guess he told my sister he won't speak to me until I am completely done with Ali. Which is fair. He doesn't deserve this. He deserves so much more! Ali and I have come to some sort of mutual agreement, for now. I just can't hate him. I don't want to. I remember when all I wanted from Ali was for him to get his shit straight with Marisol. Now all Sam wants is for me to get my shit straight with Ali. It's funny, the full circle there. Seriously, starting Monday, there will be some serious changes with me. Sam pointed out some very valid points. He tells me the truth, even if I never talk to him again. These are improvements intended to support my happiness, not his. I'm telling you, he is something so rare. I have got to get him back! I will Here is a Goal list for the first time:

<u>Three month Goal To-do-List:</u>
Quit Smoking
Start the GED process
Get a real Job
Divorce Ali
Start business with Anthony
Start being on time
Stop whiteley lying
~~Stay sex free till Sam comes back~~
Start eating healthier. Seriously, 3x's a day!
Go to a doctor. Both kinds
Start Yoga
Quit private bad habits
learn a more appropriate approach to confrontation
become completely happy with myself
talk to my distant family members
buy a car

fix my truck
write more/record more
take voice lessons
get over my stage fear
have a party just for me
make some friends so I can have a party
learn better money management skills
Stop smoking so much weed
~~*Get Sam and the kids back*~~

Love, Sophia Nahlah Saber

April 16, 2006

I went job hunting on Monday. Well, everyone flaked out on me... Daniel and Anthony! My best friend was out of town, so I called Ali. A last resort. As he was dropping me off for the interview at Costco, guess who walked out? Sam. I couldn't believe it! How could he have been there?! Then he had to walk right in front of us. The look of sheer disappointment shot from his eyes like lasers into my soul! I melted inside. How could he, of all people, be the one crossing right in front of us?! WTF?! Later, I tried to explain myself, but he was so stubborn. He said, he knows what he saw, and what he saw was enough for him. Why Sam? Why do you only just see my crap?! I want you! Furthermore, since we were both there at the same time, we should have just been together! I miss him so much! I will get over being hurt by him, but I will never get over him. He is just too good for me, I guess. Later Love, Me

May 2, 2006

Hey. I am so sick of this shit! Trying to be cool with Ali, forgetting about a normal, cool future with Sam. I WANT

TO BE ALONE! JUST ALONE!! I hate men and everything they stand for! The lies, the life they take. It all fucking sucks! I am getting used to being alone and enjoying my time. All these years, I have failed to realize one thing: I am most powerful on my own. I can move fast if I can just get a job. I could make new friends, get a new life, re-invent myself, and get those voice lessons. Then everybody can hear what I say. I am going to let me just be me. Over time, I have tried to be wifey, but I failed miserably. I give up. It's the single life for me. Until I find myself, and I am happy with just being me. Then, I can make someone else happy. In return, allowing them to make me smile about life. Love Always, Sophia N. Saber

I realized that starting a new relationship before you completely end an old one is a ridiculous ordeal. I did really think I loved Sam, but more than loving him, I think I loved what I felt when he was around. I loved to be in love, that is for sure, but I always wanted to be alone. It takes so much to stand on your own. I still had some growing to do.

I let some time pass, but not too much. I was able to wiggle my way out of the drama of these men to explore something else that had caught my attention. A little birdie. She kept chirping on my windowsill until I could no longer ignore her song. I was angry, yes, but interest in her was separate from that. It didn't matter if I was angry at men or not. I was interested in her, for her. I was also ready to defy my religious instincts, and see where that led.

May 5, 2006

Happy Cinco De Mayo! My parents would have 22 years under their belts, were it not for divorce. Thank the lord I didn't have children with Ali. Anyway, this entry should be nice and long! I have done some interesting things in the last couple of days...

...May 3, 2006

Hey you! How are you? Me, I'm fine. I have been kicking it with my friend and his sister, Mariah. Well, it was her birthday on Wednesday... Wait- go back even further...

...May 2, 2006

Hey there, you! Today, I went to Anthony and Daniel's house to smoke and say what's up. The weather is changing, so it's all hot and nice out. Anthony wanted to go to the park or do something outside, so we went on a bike ride, without Daniel. He was acting like a little biatch! He had ulterior motives. He had planned on stealing you and reading you!! Anyway, we rode around Bear Creek a few times. It was the best feeling I have had in quite some time! It's the best "date" I've ever been on! Anyway, Anthony took me home, and Daniel called me,

"Oh Sophia, you left your diary here. It must have fallen out of your bag or something." BULL-MUTHA-FUCKIN-SHIT! Yo- there is no fucking way that happened! Dude, I was so fucking pissed! So, I called Anthony, because I trust him. He got it back for me... Now, onto May 3ʳᵈ.

...May 3, 2006

Hey you, how are you? I'm fine. I had an interview at Gottschalks today. I got the job! Floor manager in the children's department. It's so good to have a job! Anyway, after that, I went home to change, then went off to Wah Sings for Chinese food for Mariah's birthday. Mariah is the fucking shit, dude! Hella cool. She is gay. I don't want to like her.

but I do. So, I'll have to stay away for a little while. Anyway, Anthony, Daniel, and their friend Trek came to play pool with us. It was so much fucking fun! I played Madonna on the Jukebox... I about emptied the place. Whatever, bitches don't know good music. It was freaking hilarious! Anthony was cracking up! He said it was cute. He's cute. After that, I was supposed to have some drinks with Mariah and her brother at the local bar. Wednesday night is karaoke night. It was hella fun! I'll let the pictures speak for the night. I was so fucking drunk, it's nuts! I could hardly walk!

Mariah and I laid on my bed, and flew through space in the stars on my ceiling. It was so fucking dope. We were supposed to go back to her house to take Jello shots for her birthday. Soya was going to meet us there so he could read some of my writing, not my writing in you, but my song lyrics. Oh yeah, we also had mad thumb wars in the dark and just laughed our asses off together. Such a breath of fresh air, you have no idea! Anyway, since I couldn't leave to go drink with her, I promised I'd make up for it the next night. So...

...May 4, 2006

Hey there, you! How are you doing? Me? Fine, just chillin. I went to work, and Ali came to give me a ride home. I got home, changed, and called Mariah to let her know I would be late. She was cool with it. Anyway, there was this super annoying girl there who Mariah and I cussed out! Shit was fun.

...May 8, 2006

...[...]...Anyway Mariah and I. My best friend and I spent all day listening to her music. This girl is beyond talented. I did my best friend's hair over at her house, we smoked a few blunts, then came to babysit for my sister. Sunday, I woke up and fought with Ali. Then I ditched that ass to go to the

lake with Mariah. But the lake was bunk, so we rolled some blunts, went back to Mariah's, sat around the fire, roasted marshmallows, and ate hot dogs. Well, I bought some jäger and red-bull. Mariah and I had decided to walk home so we could "talk to each other." There were definitely feelings beyond friendship that we thought we should discuss over a bottle of jäger, so we walked the miles toward home. We were so goddamn drunk, I don't remember half the conversation. 3/4 the way home, we started making out like crazy! I couldn't help it. Something inside of her is what's inside of me, and it pulls like magnets. It's a super heavy attraction. She is so beautiful. There is the beautiful bright light that shines through her. And she can sing like a bird! Her voice is amazing! Her words are meaningful! I don't know. I can tell, she and I are going to be very close. Even though we made out or whatever. We are the same. So, if things don't work, then we will still always be friends. I can tell. Peace out, homie! Sophia N. Saber

Hold up, Let me take the mic. Sophia isn't telling the whole story. -MC

Let's rewind it back. The day I met her, I went to a BBQ my cousin had invited me to at a property he managed. I went with my older brother and we both noticed her right away. She was breathtaking. Something out of one of those dream girl fantasies. My brother introduced himself and she came over and introduced herself to me. Her and my brother exchanged numbers. I was just hoping I'd see her again. She ended up hanging at my apartment with my brothers and a group of friends. She fascinated me. I wanted to know everything about her, but treaded lightly. I knew my brother, like myself, was deeply intrigued.

A friend of mine was having a party one day, and I invited my brother and some friends. He invited her. I brought my drink of choice (*jäger*) to the party. We all arrived together and I introduced everyone to the crew I brought. Little did I know, the girl I had been dating who had cheated on me would be at that very party. I was upset and wanted to leave. I felt bad because I brought everyone with me, but I knew I had to go.

When I told the people I came with that I wasn't comfortable being there and wanted to leave, everyone agreed it wasn't a cool place to be. That's when she (Sophia) told me to grab the bottle I bought. I was hesitant, that's not my style, but she grabbed it before I could even decide if I wanted to or not, and told me she and I were going to walk home. It was not a quick walk home, but she refused to take no for an answer.

My brother drove alongside of us and told us to get in the car, but she said no, she said we were gonna walk. So we did. We started walking, drinking, and talking. I felt so taken by her, and just followed her lead. We drank the entire bottle in a couple of miles, so we stopped at a liquor store and got more! Neither of us needed anymore to drink, but we were committed to the adventure at hand. After enough alcohol to induce courage and deep conversation, she kissed me.

It was so unexpected to me, but when it happened, I felt my lips were meant to be on hers. We talked, we walked, we drank, we kissed. We kissed so much. She would walk a bit, and I would stop, while she continued. I would wait for her to come back for me, and then I'd wait for her to kiss me again before walking. It took a long time to get back to my house. That was our beginning. What a beginning it was. I knew she had never been with a woman, and I was already in a complicated situation with one, so I took her lead. She definitely leads.

We could not stay away from each other, although we were in our own complex relationships, we didn't care. We spent every waking moment we could together. We would try to stay apart, but the same day would end up in each other's arms. Her kisses felt different, her presence felt different. I didn't want to love her, but did right away. It only grew every time I saw her.

We never judged each other, we were just in the moment we created when we were together. I've never felt someone get me so effortlessly, and I somehow knew she felt the same way. We had so many adventures. So many moments that will forever be some of the best memories of my life. Although, we eventually grew apart in some ways, and we live separate lives, anytime we see each other that magnetic feeling still burns. So, while she's downplaying all this a little– she knew what she wanted and how to get it. Whatever *it* was, is certainly not love lost.

Mic drop★ MC out.

May 10, 2006

> *Today is different. I woke up next to her, and something felt so, "ok." We get along, and click-click. That's us, we don't just click, we 'click-click.' I don't exactly know what all this means. But I like how I feel when she is around. She came to my sister's house last night to hang out with me and my nieces. Inevitably, we made out 73% of the time. NOT IN FRONT OF THE KIDS! I don't know how I feel about the whole lesbian thing yet. So we are taking it slow. I feel like I have known her for years. We have so much in common. We're both singers, the same type of artists. Except she has been doing it for ten years. I am only nine years and eight months behind. Haha. She can guide me, really help me grow and develop as an artist. I'm stoked, you have no idea, we are both extreme potheads. We smoked like two ounces already. We like listening to the same music. Some*

off the hook shit. She took me to work and played me "A Song For You, " by Donny Hathaway. The thing is, the version by Leon Russel is my favorite song. If I am going to get into a relationship with her, I am going to have to learn how to get along better with other girls. She only has guy friends... I am so excited about her. I am so lucky someone so beautiful came into my life and will stay forever. She says I am the guy. I agree. She knows who daddy is. Anyway, enough about that. Sam and I spoke for about three hours yesterday. He doesn't get me, he doesn't see the beauty that is inside of me. Or, maybe he sees it, and just has a hard time accepting it. I would still give Sam a try, but Mariah makes me feel like I'm worth much more. I still need to get over my marriage. I don't want to write too much about him, he did something recently to hurt me. Worse than before. It was the night Mariah and I were walking around drunk. I ended up staying at her house. Ali called and said he was taking my shit and breaking stuff. I ignored it. I thought he was just bluffing. I got home the next day around 6:00, only to discover that he had my three big photo albums, which coincide with my writing. He burned all of my poetry and my notebook. You know the one. A part of me died that day. I will never forgive him for this. Never. From now on life is going to be new...fresh...the sky's my limit. I can do anything I want to fucking do. I have to start loving myself again. That is the only way. Love Always, Sophia Nahlah Saber

Mariah and I don't have an exact ending to our chapter, and the story might feel light weighted. First, we're looking at a quick three months of what, at the time, seemed to be the most important thing in the world, my love life. It's light and heavy and short but significant. Mariah wasn't an experiment. Rather, something more naturally occurring at that age. We are seeking knowledge of self, and sexuality is part of the self. I was curious about sexuality and experimenting with intimacy. Building a relationship with a woman was much easier than doing so with a man. Having sex with a man (for me) was easier than sex with a woman. That was my conclusion.

I knew I could fall in love with a woman, but that I was not sexually interested. This led to our romantic story's conclusion. The sexual tension would never be resolved any other way than with action, an action I just couldn't bring myself to demonstrate. Whether from the fear of religious repercussions, or a negative interaction with my mother, or the instance from when I was 15. I was making a decision and standing by it. Because Mariah provided such an open space for me to explore myself in an authentic way, we are able to manage a long and healthy relationship.

Looking back now, this was just the beginning of a life-long evolutionary exploration of self and sexuality. When Kinsey said sexuality was on a sliding scale, he knocked it out of the park. No one is 100% anything 100% of the time. However, I was 100% sure my marriage was over, and that I was really ready to move forward. I was rebounded and connected to a deeper part of my feminine divine and sexuality. While I still didn't have everything figured out, and perfect, and shiney, I was making progress toward my future.

CHAPTER 8

Cocaine For Breakfast

Noun: *an addictive drug derived from coca or prepared synthetically, used as an illegal stimulant and sometimes medicinally as a local anesthetic.*

May 11, 2006

> *Hey there, you. I had a pretty interesting night last night. Anthony and Daniel talked me into going to a hip-hop thing, even though I hate crowds. My best friend was supposed to accompany me, but she backed out at the last minute, so I went alone. I was looking damn good. However, I noticed I was the only one looking the way I did. Rap shows are much different than the club. I was there for the experience of the show. I found DJ ICE. He was at his merch table selling shirts. He called me over to the table and told me I had won the contest for being the best at the show. He gave me a free shirt and blah blah blah. The event was tight! DJ ICE was hella cool! I have nothing but good shit to say about him! But the reality of Ali just hit. He is gone forever. I love you, fat guy, one last time. -Sophia*

That was the night I met one of the most influential loves of my lifetime. I met Ice when I was having a rough night. I was in the middle of my divorce, and getting over my rebound, while still dealing with new feelings of feminine romantic attraction. I was definitely not looking for anything that night. I just wanted to be out.

Ice had called me over to his merch table after the show, but only because I had positioned myself directly in his eyesight. I wanted to be called over. I had never seen any man like him. He was confident, and tatted the fuck up. His laugh was enormous, and he smiled so easily. He also seemed to take notice of me. I traced my fingers along all the CD's on his merch table and settled on the one called *La Vida Loca*. I loved it because it was colorful and playful, and seemed like it would be easy to listen to. I found it very creative.

I only wanted to flirt, so after we talked about our tattoos and I got my CD, I left outside to smoke and he followed me. I stood with my foot flat against the wall, making a pattern 4 with my legs. I had a few drinks in me, so I was somewhat emotional.

"Hey, why are you sneaking around here? I see you sneaking upstairs during the show to watch by yourself. Why do you do that?"

"I like to be alone, I guess. Besides, I feel really out of place here."

"Weird, but ok. I can dig it. You look out of place, for sure. Did you know where you were going when you got dressed?"

"I just thought I was going out. I have never been to a hip hop show, so I guess I didn't."

"What's your story?" He asked, through innocent laughter.

"I'm 21 and in the middle of a divorce. You?"

"Ahhh, so you're not your typical 21 year old?"

"No, I am not."

"How would you like to come back to my hotel with me?"

"Haha! I wouldn't, not even a little bit!"

"What?! But I thought we were feeling each other?"

"You can come to my place, I don't do the hotel thing. That's for sure. But one thing- No plans. No Sex."

"No sex? No plans? Ok deal."

He finished his set, and Daniel gave us a ride to my house. The whole way, Daniel lectured me on girls who take home artists, and what happens to them. I wasn't hearing any of it. When we arrived at my house, we played bones for hours. I whooped his ass the whole time, or so he let me think. We talked a lot about the music industry, my family, upbringing, and such. I don't remember the evening perfectly, but I remember taking my shirt off without hesitation once we decided it was time for bed. Once we had exhausted the bones, movies, and conversation, we climbed into bed together. Mariah called, I answered. While we were talking, he was teasing me. But really just working himself up, so I let him cum on my chest. I felt as though I had to let him, I had been teasing him all night, too. But "no sex, no plans" was in full effect. I was instantly in like with this cool-bad dood.

May 22, 2006

> *Hi. His name is DJ ICE. He is the main DJ for a Rap group. Since he left my house that morning after the show, there hasn't been a day that has gone by without me hearing his voice. He actually came back to town just to see me. As soon as he got off tour, he jumped on Amtrak and hit up Merced, just for me. I picked him up around 10:00 pm. I had the girls and two other kids. I was babysitting that night. I didn't know he was going to take to the girls so well. I liked that he was so fucking cute with them. I didn't like how he made me feel, like I could really fall for him. This is all for now. Mariah is here so we can write. Love, Sophia N. Saber*

May 25, 2006

> *HAPPY BIRTHDAY SISTER! Hey you, I have a really good reason for not writing to you for so long. ICE. He's got*

my mind turning over like 100 x's a second! I am going to
copy all of his text messages for you to understand.

I recorded his text messages because it was the amount
of effort this man put in to gain my attention that ultimately
won me over. Back in this day and age, technology hadn't yet
developed into text threads. On a Nokia phone, you had hard
buttons with numbers. On each number were three letters.
Depending on which word you were spelling, you might have
to click a button up to three times to get a single letter of the
word you're trying to spell. It was a whole process.

Texting back then, was not as easy or accessible as it is
now. With the spelling of each word, I was falling for his
effort, for the love that he was starting to dedicate to me.
I made the effort of hand recording it in my diary. As I
mentioned, I didn't have access to my replies because they
were kept in a different folder, and if you had texted multiple people, you would have to really dig. I always wanted to
remember his efforts. I read his words often throughout our
relationship; to this day reading them makes me warm.

5/12/06

ICE: *Why can't I stop thinking about you?!*
ICE: *I see you falling deeply for a dope-ass DJ from LA, and I see you getting*
     out of Merced to capture all of your dreams. I also see the two of you
     having many worldly adventures and more fun than you ever dreamed
     possible.

5/13/06

ICE: *let's get free, you are going to have to take down the wall around your*
     heart first.
ICE: *You don't know what you're getting yourself into Baby*

5/14/06

ICE: *Get at me when you slip on the queen Bee's and a wife beater, I want to taste you.*

ICE: *Hey, I wanna talk to yo ass.*

ICE: *Now I am sad.*

ICE: *Can I have your cake and eat it too???*

ICE: *Sophia bath water on the rocks please.*

ICE: *Listen up Sophia, do you really think all I want is one night?*

ICE: *That is a question full of layers. There is almost nothing you could say to scare me off. i.e.: I know you are married and your almost ex-husband is a little psycho. I know that a lot of your homies are fans of my crew, you live in crazy ass Merced and you have a girlfriend. What do I want from you? hummmmm. Unconditional brutal honesty & respect. Possibility of seriousness in the future and the best sexual adventures we both have ever experienced.*

5/15/2006

ICE: *Made it back to the telly. I want you.*

ICE: *Good night princess, if you keep reaching for me, eventually, I will end up in your arms. Where I belong. Mwah★*

ICE: *I am thinking about you...so know that and multiply this text by 20,000...then you will find you are on my mind an average of every 8.5 seconds. I hope the abundant range of thoughts doesn't frighten you. Mwah★*

ICE: *I think about how much falling in love is unavoidable.*

ICE: *So you wanna be my woman huh?*

ICE: *It's on you baby, I am surprised you ain't feeling the realness here. I meet women all the time, but this is so different.*

ICE: *Don't be scared, choose life, love and happiness.*

5/17/2006

ICE: *Are you being honest?*

ICE: *You want me huh? What do you want to do to me?*

ICE: *Fine then, duck the question.*

ICE: *Stop ignoring my humble request and share the information baby.*

ICE: *Daaaaaaaaaaaaaamn. Vividly depicted & Painted. You just told the future baby. I got you.*

ICE: *I am coming to chill for sure*

5/18/2006

ICE: *Ummmmm*

ICE: *There was nothing wrong until the last call's exit. Ugggghhh, but before it was just me wanting you to know that you can say anything to me vs. the locals...ie: your girlfriend/husband or etc... I wasn't tripping, I just caught myself catching feelings when you said you kissed ol' girl the other day. I was wondering which lovey dovey text you did that between! But that's sucka shit...I wish I never flinched. Resume normal activities now.*

ICE: *I miss your eyes, and your hair down all wild and shit! Call me later my sleek little panther* I am on my way.*

5/19/06

ICE: *I will be booking my flight today...now what?!*

ICE: *I wanna know you inside and out and vice versa.*

ICE: *You can tell me anything and everything, I want to learn!*

ICE: *You are too cute and oh yah- i am going back to Cali, cali- cali!*

ICE: *Why? Are you thinking of meeting me there?*

ICE: *Well, do we wait till June? I say Nah.*

ICE: *How baby, gimme a realistic answer.*

ICE: *Merced isn't on the way, baby. But you have my brain and heart working overtime.*

ICE: *Awh! I smell a power couple.*

5/22/06

ICE: *I want to consume your days/nights*
ICE: *I miss you more, and this leaving you? Is some old bullshit.*

5/23/06

ICE: *That text got me rock hard. I need to be with you now! Meet me in Alaska.*
ICE: *I wanna hear you moaning and purring my little sleek panther.*
ICE: *Duh! Why would ICE get to have his cake and eat it too? I'll be good as long as you are being better, keeping it warm, tight and wetter. (Hey that rhymed!)*
ICE: *And you said you would let me eat the cake, you nasty.*
ICE: *You make a muFCKA wanna pass up some show dough.*

5/25/06

ICE: *Have a great day you!*
ICE: *How about you hear my voice in your ear while I talk to you during the best sex of your life?*
ICE: *Why do you mean so much to me already? Not fair.*
ICE: *Speak Damnit.*
ICE: *No pic sent. If you wanna talk to me just say so I will call you.*

5/26/06

ICE: *Stop sending me texts that are meant for other people. I'm signing off.*

5/27/06

ICE: *I am about to take off. I love talking to you around the clock. wherever/ whenever*
ICE: *I hope that text was for me.*

ICE: *I'm calling you when I get to the gate, man I wish I was flying into Fresno.*

ICE: *Answer your phone when I call..okaaaaaaay!*

ICE: *Bring you a bagel?! WTF?! I know that text wasn't for me Sophia. Uggghhh*

ICE: *You are very perceptive, and now I feel like a jealous creep. I'm sorry baby. Jealousy is whack! Of course, I will get you that bagel, and that guy that tried to holla at you when I left... he kind of looked like me. Oxoxox*

ICE: *I wanna see you badly!*

ICE: *I would fly out of LAX, and what's my return date?*

ICE: *You really want me out there that long?*

ICE: *Your plan is cool, if $350 is the best price then that's me. Also, I am considering just taking a rain check on it all.*

ICE: *yeah, I've thought it over and I've decided that maybe I wasn't meant to go. Hopefully the regret and misery of not being where I want to be will inspire some dope writing and recording. I want to see you whenever you have time for me.*

5/30/06

ICE: *Colorado is calling me! What should ICE do?! Xoxox*

ICE: *Ain't that the truth! Hmmmm*

ICE: *Flattery will get you everywhere.*

ICE: *You are adorable.*

May 30, 2006

> *Hey there, you! Do you understand now why I have not been writing?! I have had nothing to write. Look, I know that the last thing I need right now is another serious relationship. I don't know for sure that that's what this is. But it could definitely go there. And do you see why?! He has them words! Really, I don't know shit about him except he has a set of twins and a daughter with two two baby mama's.*

One lives in Kansas, one lives in London. GODDAMN. But for some reason, I am more than willing to overlook the bullshit. He seems to be what I have been looking for. He says I am everything he has been looking for while not looking. I want to take a chance, let my heart go for love's sake. Seems like I have had so much heartbreak recently, I don't know how much heart I have left. Feels like he leans over my heart with a thread and a needle mending the broken parts with potential love for me. It's exhilarating! I feel life filling my once lifeless soul. I've finally learned not to think every man is "the one." Anyway, I have more to tell you, but the kids are all waking up from their naps. Love, Sophia

June 6, 2006

I don't know exactly how much I have told you, but I am out here in CO right now, with my brother and dad. Things are so different around here. My brother is all grown up and my dad is super depressed. I wonder how things got this way? Time has passed and age has set in for both of them. ICE is coming in on Wednesday to meet them. He and I are basically a unit now and we are sure of it. I wonder how he and my dad will react to one another. I wonder how my dad is going to react to my "DJ boyfriend" Anyway, I'll catch you up on everything tomorrow. I love you with all that is me. Sophia

June 7, 2006

Hey there, you! How are you? Me, I am fine. Good, really. My dad and I went to pick up ICE from the airport yesterday. Then we had a really long talk about my childhood, about my mom, why she did some of the things she has, and why she hates me so much. My dad says it's not my fault, she was raised in womanizing Kuwait and she doesn't know

any better. Even though he hates her, I can tell he still puts
it so poetically. I'm out. Sophia

June 16, 2006

Hey, I need some lyrical inspiration. Something is blocking
my writing genius. ICE! Has taken my mind to new levels,
a new place. He has lifted me off the dirty ground and has
my head in the clouds! Lifted so high..so so high. Ironically,
that's all I have to say. Love always, SNS

June 20, 2006

Hey there, you! How come in the last month I have taken
the most monumental steps in my short 21 years of life, and
I can't fucking write about it?! I just had to stop by to say hi.

Obviously Ice and I had met up in Colorado. He met my father and they instantly fell in love with each other. He was becoming more important to me than any other man could even dream to be. Ice was different. He was a man who had been around the world. He exercised his brain and made his own decisions based on critical thought. He did what he wanted to do. I was in love.

We were two months in, going on 18 years. I couldn't write because he had taken the place of my writing. I was using all my communicative energy on and with him. We talked and texted so often I didn't need to write about it. I was too busy living it and enjoying him and our time to-gether. We both wanted more out of it, and we wanted it quickly.

After Colorado, I went back to Mercede and he went off to his next show. He sent for me to come visit in July. We went on our first date in LA. He didn't have a set plan, but he was able to tell me to ask him for anything, so I did.

"Anything?" I said.

"Yes. Anything."

"OK. I want a Ferris Wheel"

I had tried so hard to think of something that was seasonal or only came into town with the carnies. He told me to close my eyes and 15 minutes later, after a very fun car ride, I opened my eyes to Santa Monica Pier. I was so blown away, I began to cry. He said anything, and he meant it. I knew then he was my man, he would truly do anything for me. We had the best day ever, just messin' around on the boardwalk, boat rides, and laughter. We were falling in love just enjoying one another and the boardwalk.

July 28, 2006

> *Oh my love! Hey you. How have you been? Lonely as fuck, I am sure. Sorry, I've been away for so long. I have been traveling and, yes, I cheated on you. So sorry, my love. Poetry is her name, and she lives in my pink notebook. You know this journey I have been on to "find myself?" Well, I went on one for real. I have not really been home since May. I've been to Colorado: Lafayette, Boulder, Denver. California: Santa Cruz, LA (South Central and Hollywood). Nevada: Carson City, Reno. But enough about my travels, let's finally talk about ICE. So, all you know so far is the text messages, and I had stopped recording just before I left for Colorado. Time for me in the last three months has just been a blur. I am in Reno right now, just waking up at the Greyhound station. The bus I was supposed to be on at 8:00 pm filled up, so I had to have an adventure last night. I'm gonna get out of here. Later. Love, Sophia*

August 1, 2006

> *Hey there, love, how are you? Me? I'm super! Big cheese!*
> *I'm on a train from Merced to LA, to go see ICE. It's his*
> *28th birthday tomorrow. I was supposed to leave last night,*
> *but I lost my ticket right before I was supposed to leave!*
> *So, I had to wait until today. Ok, so here it is. I left for*
> *Colorado via airplane early June. Well, late May, it was an*
> *issue whether or not ICE was coming, but questions were*
> *answered and he came.*

August 4, 2006

> *Hey, beautiful! Out of all my very limited artistic abili-*
> *ties, you are my favorite. True, honest, passion. I love it!*
> *Anyway, I'm on the Amtrak bus, on my way home. This*
> *trip out here was different. When he picked me up from the*
> *bus station, he took me to a place called "Melrose." I guess*
> *it's a shopping street. I was looking for something to wear*
> *for his birthday. So, I was taking my time. Well, he was all*
> *cracked out on cocaine. Coming down. I could smell it all*
> *over him. He took the heat and exercised like a champ! We*
> *walked from store to store looking for something, finally we*
> *found a little black number that we both loved. So, we went*
> *home. As I am getting ready, he comes into the living room*
> *where I was doing my make-up and practiced his set for the*
> *Roxy tonight. Then he says, "Sophia, I have something to*
> *tell you- I lied to you about something." My heart sank. I*
> *didn't know what was coming after that statement. "I actu-*
> *ally have four kids," He says. "She lives in Atlantic City*
> *and she is six." I believed him. The same feeling that I got*
> *when I found out Marisol was pregnant washed over me. I*
> *had dumped him in two seconds! Only in my head. I said ab-*
> *solutely nothing and held back my tears so as not to give away*
> *how I really felt. After a moment of silence he demanded I*

speak. I said, "I am still waiting for you to tell me what is going on." He started laughing! Phew! He was just yanking my chain. However, I remained completely unprepared for what came next. I misunderstood and overreacted. He said... "I am 37, not 28." I wouldn't have minded at all, you see. But when we were in Reno we had a brief discussion about his age. He asked if he was older would I mind? Of course not, I had thought. Just mad that he had lied about that or just even at all. Now he was coming clean. We met May 10th, it is now August 3rd. He has been lying this whole time and doing a good job at it. So what other skeletons did he have hung in his closet? At first, I was just so relieved that he didn't have another secret child. Or does he?! I hate this! I want to trust the man I am with completely. And now his honesty is slightly tainted. But, it's really no big deal. So, he's 37, not 28. And??? But now I am dealing with a much bigger issue. He is past thirty and continues to do things a man should not do. Player days are for young and stupid men. Even a 27 year old can get away with that shit. Not a 37 year old! His anger should have somewhat subsided by now. His irrational fear of Mariah shouldn't exist. He should want to spend more time with his kids- or well, no. I can't knock him there, he seems to be a great father. I just haven't seen him in action. Anyway, I find myself constantly questioning his maturity and ability to love & respect me as a woman. There is a flip side to all of this madness. He is 37, so that explains why he is so smart, why he has three kids, why he controls his life, why he owns his own company, why he is so jealous! And why he has something to say about EVERYTHING! And why he is always right. I don't know, this whole age thing needs time. Anyway, I finished getting ready and I looked great, until you got to my feet. Oh, my poor, ugly feet. He tried to get me shoes to match my dress, but they were all open-toed. Nope. Can't do it.

We ended up taking some wack ass e-pills and did our best
to be social. Then we went home and had GREAT sex till
the sun came up. Then, we slept till 2:00 pm the next day.
On his birthday, we went to the beach and had the most fun
I've had in years, playing in the sand and getting wiped out
by the waves. Then he had to stick his stupid hand in the
stupid sand and throw stupid gray sand crabs at me! He gave
me crabs! It was an absolutely beautiful day. Love, Sophia
N. Saber

Reading how judgemental I was toward him because of his age, or any other matter is laughable. Here I was, with nothing in life except words on pages and a trail of tears behind me, and *I* was judging *him*. This seems so out of pocket to me, but I'll forgive it. I had just learned that there was a substantial age difference between us and I did feel a bit trapped. But what's more, is that this was the beginning of where our trust issues stem.

However, it wasn't enough of a deal breaker for me to leave, not this. Not the kids he already had, not the fact that I was still legally married, and not that I had no planned future of my own. Like he said, both our mama's tried to warn us, but we promised that we want us.

August 11, 2006

Hey there, you! About two weeks ago, I went into a pho-
tography/creative studio run by a very edgy photographer.
I went in with no makeup on my face. And I was coming
down from some heavy drugs (cocaine). I had never been in
front of a professional camera before. I thought it was like
my camera, but more expensive. Here's what happens: there
is a shutter speed, so it takes 35 pictures a second, and I get
to move around while I'm shooting. It captures the best and
the worst. The pictures came out beautifully. A week later, I

*was assigned my first gig in Monterey, California. =) Love,
Sophia N. Saber*

August 14, 2006

*So, this modeling thing. The shoot was fun. About 400-
500 pictures were taken and I only got to see 7-8 of them.
I look good, but my photographer doesn't think so, with all
the photoshop he uses! BOO! I almost broke up with ICE
last night, we fought too much.*

September 22, 2006

*Hey there, you. Stranger. Stranger in my life. My life
changed. ICE has changed my life, not just him. We have
changed my life. As of now, I practically live with him in
LA. It's weird. All the goals I have ever had in life are going
to, or have already come true next to my man. I have been
with him consecutively since September 1st. That's when I
drove from Merced to Oakland to meet him for a broke-ass
summer jam. When I got there, we had a pretty serious
conversation. I was radiant that night, I have to look my best
for him. He is the star shining on the stage, I have to shine
equally as bright for him. I can too. I hadn't had sex with
my man in a few days. After a much needed trip to Walmart
and a shower, we got it on like donkey kong!*

September 23, 2006

*Hey, you! Look, I've been out here, or just haven't gone
home for 22 days now. My rent is about to be three months
late. I still don't have a job. ICE is paying for everything.
Everything. I can't do this to him, or me, for very much
longer. My endeavor home begins on Monday, when I return
home it's a job and a divorce! I am feeling so guilty lately.*

ICE deserves better than what I have been able to give to him. I'm afraid if I don't step up, I will lose him. He has shown me what my life can be with him. He asked me to marry him on September 11. I accepted. Hm. My first actual engagement. Even after I cheated on him. He is sure about his love for me. It's almost scary. I constantly question the authenticity. Love Always, Sophia N. Saber

November something, 2006

Hi. I have never been so upset and confused. I am 21, I'm still married. But I have been separated for almost ten months, seven of which I have been with ICE. I know you don't know much about him, that's because he says it all. He is perfect. He shows genuine human nature, he understands something about life that only a handful of people ever hope to understand. He has a strong magnetic personality that draws everybody to him. Even people you wouldn't expect to. Like my father, who LOVES him. Of course Anthony and Daniel love him, they are life long fans. Anyway, I really like him and I like to be around him. But I feel like he hates me. He is a very intelligent human being, therefore he thinks his life out. He has set up a life plan totally to his liking. He is living his dream. Less than a handful of people are actually doing that. He has a huge vocabulary! Huge! He can out talk me no matter what! And he is always right!!! I mean literally, he has been wrong maybe twice. I cheated first. Yes. We were in our second or third month. Ali and I had been split for almost five months. He was scrambling for me still, even though I had clearly moved on. Or had I? I was clearly confused about ICE in the beginning. Is he a good guy or a bad guy?!I couldn't tell. He has this thing where he told me about his past, all his wrong doings. Well, just what he wanted me to know. A cheat? I will never know. Love, Sophia N. Saber

November 29, 2006

Hey there, you! I am on a plane on my way to Portland, Oregon. You want to know why? I work for ICE now. I'm a "merch girl." So, I sat at the booth with all of the band's goodies. I sell it for them during and after the show. It's not my dream job, but the perks are unbelievable. I couldn't even tell you how many planes I have been on in the past seven months. Colorado, Wisconsin, Oakland, Atlanta, Copenhagen, Santa Barbara, SFO, Oregon...the list continues, shows and merch, and one of the most powerful relationships I will ever be in. The intensity of passion and reliance is high, very high. Speaking of high, you know I am a pothead, right? Well, ICE super caters to my weed habit. I asked him why he kept me so weeded out, he said he likes me better when I'm stoned. That hella hurt. He said he was playing...but I still believed it as truth. Anyway, I officially moved out here Friday. He spent $400.00 for a Uhaul. Helped me pack all my shit in Merced then drove me down to LA. Actually, I drove, but that is neither here nor there. He came and got me. Everything he said he would do for me. He did. He almost never breaks his promises to me. He is really good to me. Ok, we're taking off now. Bye. Love, Sophia

December 4, 2006

Hey, you! ICE and I fit in a cosmically correct way. I wrote a prophetic entry on April 27th, 2006. Before I even met him. Crazy! He fulfills my dreams and makes me close to the happiest I have ever been. He told me he loved me only four weeks after knowing me. How? Why? He told me at my dad's house by tractor. I thought he meant it, exactly why it scared the shit out of me. Ice obviously sees who I am inside. But how could he, after only four weeks of bliss? He is nothing less than amazing! An answer to my life long

*prayers. There is a flip side, he is 37 and a grown-ass man.
I am still a child. He helps me grow. Anyway, for as much
passion that we love each other with, we also hate each other
with the same intensity. Ice and I are more alike than anyone
on this planet, yet we are total and complete opposites. SNS*

December 11, 2006

*Hey, you! I can't believe some of the things I am about to
say. So, since I have met ICE, we have been pretty much
inseparable, right. My life when he met me was so different.
It may not have been so glamorous and popular, but I had
friends. You know, those people you talk to. I miss Sancha.
You can't just look for a new best friend or even replace an
old one. No matter how far away from each other we are,
she and her son will always have a special place in my heart.
I haven't seen my nieces in a while either. They give my
life purpose. Without them, I am nothing. I don't have a
phone yet. I can't afford it. Ice doesn't want to pay for one.
That's ok, but it just cut me off from a lot of people. The
whole myspace thing is a joke. Every time I try to get on
it he calls me a "myspace whore," his exact words. Cause
I am soooooooooo special. Anyway, here is what is hurting
me. Before I moved out here, I told him that I desperately
needed to go clothes shopping. Not just for vanity purposes,
but because my clothes are cheap and old. Since I was moving to LA, I asked him if he could take me around to the
bargain spots, Ross, Marshalls...etc. I was coming with a
note, and then it fell through. He said he would match my
money but that we had to wait till we got to Europe to do
any shopping. I thought that was so sweet of him, not too
much, and not too little. I do hate a man who spoils me.
Well, when we got there it just didn't work out. So, my
clothing situation continues to deteriorate. It's been a month
exactly! I have been saving my measly merch money so that*

I can pay for my divorce. Anyway, this morning we went to the clothing company that sponsors him. They give him free clothes every couple weeks or so to keep it fresh. He is a walking advertisement for them. But he and I are a team, and I feel so incomparable aesthetically standing next to him. He is a performer, it's definitely part of the job. I asked him if afterward he could finally go shopping for me. We hit up Ross and I got three new pairs of shoes, some new jeans, and a few shirts. However, when we got home, he called me selfish for not getting him anything. I didn't even react, I couldn't believe how he was coming at me..like I'm some kind of selfish bitch. He has everything any man could ever want! Including FREE clothes from a well-to-do company! I had to pay for mine. I just don't understand, I live for this man. I have given him my whole life and he wants me to spend my measly clothing money on him?! I am so hurt right now...who the fuck behaves like that?! He doesn't see it that way. He thinks I owe him for saving me from my wretched life, then reminding me of how great he is. When we were leaving Portland, we had separate flights so he gave me $10 to go away with. Yup, $10. Like a jr. high kid leaving campus. It's ridiculous. We were separated for two hours, and I missed that asshole! You know how I love cards? So, I got him one that said "HO-HO-HO," in honor of his second life. It wasn't too mushy, just enough to say I do love you and if you give me $10 I will spend it on your spoiled grown man ass. I got him a lucky charm and put it inside. It was a rocket ship with a heart on the tip. So we could take our love to the moon, like we promised each other. Look, I'm not making any money right now and he definitely measures love with weight. He needs a big diamond ring. I don't even like copper rings. Is my love enough for ICE? I hope he knows I love him. But again, who is going to look out for me if I don't look out for me? Love Always, Sophia N. Saber

December 12, 2006

Hey you! This year, this sweet-n-sour year of mine is almost at its end. I don't really have any kind of new year's resolutions or anything like that. But, I do have a story about today. So, we have this friend, Jaime, who does promotion work for ICE. Jaime has a messy apartment, so I told him I would deep clean it for $150.00, to replace the money I spent on shopping. I was supposed to be there around 12:00, but slept right through my alarm and multiple attempts made by ICE to wake me up. Due to our fantastic brawl we had last night that ran till 6:30 am, I couldn't wake up in time. Even when I did, our fight continued. ICE doesn't like when I talk to Jamie on the phone, he thinks that there is something between us. He is Crazy! Really, he is crazy. So, we fought some more. Both of our days were ruined, he needed to run errands, and I needed a break. So, we agreed that he would drop me off on Hollywood Blvd, so I could walk around. You know, that thing that I used to live for? WALKING! The only walking I do now is from our bedroom to the kitchen to make his sex sandwiches!

Anyway, I was so excited! I had the whole strip to myself! I could be whoever I wanted to be! I had rounded up nine dollars and some change from the house, Timothy had offered me another ten dollars. I refused it. There was a fortune teller right away, of course. He was great for nine dollars, he told me a lot about myself right away. He knew I was Palestinian. Then he said I was heart broken due to a recent pregnancy mishap. He said I would only have a daughter (someday). Then he turned my hand upside down and ran his fingers along my life line. He looked at me with such perplexion, "Young lady, how old are you?" "21, going on 22." I sharply replied. "Well, you're due into your 90's. However, your current age is showing about 30. You have had some experience with life in your short time, I see?" He talked to me about ICE for a while, said he felt he was a good man, but that my current job was a waste, and that I felt it was more of a hand out than a real job. Which it was! He was so right about that. He said, I am happiest as a self-sufficient human; less dependence was required. He said that he felt a loss. I hadn't moved to LA for the same reasons everyone else moves to the city. He said what was coming for me would find me no matter where I am at, and just to be ready to follow my call when it came. We had a great conversation, great guy. Totally worth my last nine dollars. I moved on, took some pictures, ate some food, saw a movie premier, lots of bright lights, fancy people, red carpets... My favorite part was walking, just walking. I am a walker, always have been, always will be. Love Always, SNS

January 17, 2007 (Two days after my 22nd. Birthday)

I'm pregnant. At least, that is what the test says. I smile because it is what I have always wanted. But for Timothy and I...? I'm all scrambled up inside. It's definitely the only thing I have ever really wanted, but this is his fourth time. I don't know. It's not like we didn't ask for this just two days ago. He placed his hands on my belly after he came inside me and prayed for a baby. Then we kissed to seal the deal. I guess there is a God. OMG-WTF. Love, Sophia N. Saber

January 22, 2007

Ice and I had very opposite reactions to my positive pregnancy test. He was so excited, I was distorted. I couldn't even tell you why. For as long as I could remember all I wanted to do was be a mother. Now, as a future mother, my thought is this. On January 6th, Diamond (Montana's sister), Ice, & I, all went to San Luis Obispo for a show. For the next three days we did six different heavy ass drugs, one right after another. No food breaks, no water breaks, just three days of straight rock hard drugs. We started with weed and alcohol, then someone offered us cocaine. Then we were offered Ecstasy… Then the shrooms. Finally, we dropped acid. I have nothing to say for myself. I will never do acid or shrooms again. Fuck that. I hate hallucinogens. We are not friends, thank you very much. But more importantly, I did all this with my baby developing inside my belly. How do I justify having this kid? The thought of not having this baby is tearing us apart at the seams. We are definitely on separate pages. SNS

My positive pregnancy test had thrown a wrench in our cocaine for breakfast lifestyle. I was discovering myself in a shadow cast by a very bright light. I didn't feel fully grown, not enough to then grow with someone else. I only knew where I had been, so the ideas I was having of where we were going as a couple were dismal at best. I was still questioning where he would be in ten years, and what that meant about where I could be in ten years, and I didnt like it. I couldn't imagine a future family with this man, not the way I thought my kid deserved. I still needed to learn it wasn't what I deserved either.

January 23, 2007

So, here I am, 6.5 weeks. My due date is September 13, 2007. A Virgo baby. That's not so bad. Maybe it's my boy or my girl. I just know it's not healthy, and the possibility of me keeping him or her is definitely still being discussed. I'm pregnant on the left side; he is not very nice to me. I named him Josh, after my mother's first son whom she gave up for adoption. Someday, I am going to adopt twin boys and name the eldest Josh, after him. To right the wrong, the abuse my mother, and now I, have both done. I'm so sorry for my baby, my first child that may never be. Mommy loves you baby, so does daddy.

See, baby, daddy is the only good thing in mommy's life. He loves me real good. We are best friends, and you are the addition we have been praying for. I never thought I could have you! And now that you are here, or about to be here, I am not prepared, and you are not going to be healthy. The lifestyle your father and I live involves drugs, and at your four week stage of development mommy did one of the stupidest things in her life! I took too many different drugs at once, and that will have a catastrophic effect on your development. I can't do that to you, you deserve the start of a lifetime. Trust me baby, this world is a fucked up place as is. Would you be mad if I saved another child in your place? I want to heal the world, starting with the children. Your father supports me no matter what I do. I thought you should know this. When I found out that I was pregnant with you, daddy was so excited! I did not give your father a chance to express himself, and that made him upset. All I could think about was the two weeks prior, when I had messed up any chance you had at health. I am an unhealthy person as is. I haven't eaten in almost three days, and the doctor says if I don't eat, you will just take from nutrients already present in my body...my question is WHAT FUCKING NUTRIENTS? Oops, sorry, mama curses sometimes. Kidding. Most of the time. But I'd sure watch my language once you arrived, or at least make sure you only swore at home! Ha! Kidding, again. But, alas, that day may never be. You make me throw up every day. Like, eight fucking times a day. I've waited so long for morning sickness. I love it, but I hate it. I know it's temporary. Every time I am reminded that I will never get to tell you this story. I'm sorry baby. I'm sorry mama wasn't prepared. I will get you back. I know it. I'll know when I

*see your eyes across the seas. I love you baby Josh. Daddy
does too. Love, Me*

January 24, 2007

*I'm on a train back to LA to be with my better half. That
much I know is true. I can see where Ice is the answer for
me. He has done nothing but lift me out of an early grave.
I'm horrible to him, yet he still loves me. He is amazing.
Separating from him has been one of the worst experiences
our relationship has had to endure. He wants to leave me.
Everything about me points him to leave our 'marriage.' The
cheating. The young minded person that I am. But he sees
in me what I can't see in me. That's why he can't explain
it either. He just genuinely loves me. I don't know, it is a
weird relationship for me. I am used to being the giver, you
know. Supplying my man with everything that he needs.
But Ice supplies everything I need. Weird, super strange.
But life with him is comfortable, green, and relaxing. What
exactly is it I do for him to cause his love?! I have hurt him
so many times. I wonder where he draws his strength from.
I draw mine from him. I am telling the truth about him.
About us. But we are fighting badly right now. I stayed
with Daniel when I went back home, because all my nieces
wanted to talk about was my baby. I couldn't handle it, so
I stayed with him.*

January 29, 2006

*Hey, you. I'm feeling very un-pregnant. Tomorrow is my
seventh knowledgeable week. But it seems since the beginning, an abortion is more realistic than actually becoming a
mother?! Last weekend, my sister and the girls came down to
see me. We were supposed to go to Disneyland, thank God*

we didn't tell the girls. We didn't end up going. The whole thing was a bust.

January 31, 2007

Hello, you, I have had this problem lately. It's been going on for a while. His sexuality. It's very strong, very highly driven. He abuses it the way we abuse drugs. For me, sex is for making babies. It's the physical manifestation of love. For him, sex is absolutely necessary two or three times a day if he could! I don't always feel as though he is trying to make a baby. Which, by the way, he ROCKS at baby making! Since we went to the taping of a talk show special about our friends from the Chicken Coup in Nevada, I learned more about TV, which is a hideous spectacle! This particular talk show, that is. We are friends with the girls that were interviewed, and this show made them look like shit on this earth. Who the fuck do they think they are?! Anyway, we went in a limo and he introduced me as his lubricant squeezer... really? What the fuck were we there for? We could have just met up with Tyler and the Chicks later. Anyway, he just has his 'TwoFace' today. Weird. I don't know, that's his star side. I guess I have to let it ride because it works for him. The people want that, and that's who they love. I have to share him with the public. I love him. "Insert Government name" that is, not ICE. I just accept ICE, because he comes along with loving "Government name." When we are home, just the two of us, he doesn't act a fool. That's when I love him the most. He knows that he can't really get away with that crap! It's hard for me in public. I can't and shouldn't go off on him. He has to be DJ ICE when we're out. And I don't really want to share "Govt Name," so I have to degrade and embarrass myself, and that's hard. Anyway, I know I have to leave that side alone. When he is like that, I just become his human punching bag. It's called teamwork. I still keep

him in line, I'm his woman, of course, I do. He knows better
than to piss me off too much in public places. He's almost
like a child, constantly testing boundaries and pushing my
buttons. We had a really bad fight the night before my sister
and the girls came. He grabbed scissors and embedded them
into his neck. He gets scary and violent. I don't know where
this is going anymore. PC Sophia N. Saber

At this point in my pregnancy, I had not stopped attending shows and engaging in poor behavior. I was almost sure
about the abortion, and he was either still pretending to want
a child with me, or he was sincere. I will never know. I do
know my body and mind were not aligned with his sexual
prowess, or the demands of which this environment would
expect of me. Or expect of us.

There was no way I could have survived with him down
that path. It wasn't his fault or even of his doing, just the
nature of the industry and its inescapable claws. It wasn't
just stretching my sexual limits physically, but emotionally,
as well. I was beginning to deteriorate right before him
and God.

February 1, 2007

Wow! Where did January go? Well, It's a new day and I am
keeping my baby. I know it's a boy. I can tell. It's all I have
ever wanted. How could I be so selfish? I'm going to totally
change my life for my baby. Him and I, alone. My love. It's
the only relationship I have ever wanted. I know what my
decision means for my relationship with Ice. He had baby
mama #2 come pick her mail up from the house. I dunno it
just made me think, I'm his third BM. If it's a girl, I know
he will want nothing to do with her, he already has three that
he somewhat ignores…what's a fourth? I feel this way now,
but it is still early. In the end, I want a family situation for

my children. But I could also raise them alone, with my real family. I'm not too upset with replacing Ice's male influence with my father and brother, I'm sure they won't mind. I can get a job at walgreens and we can live in the lower middle class. BM2 said she could come pick her mail up on the fifth of Feb. If he is still lying to me at this point, oh fucking well. I snooped and read his email, I guess I get what I deserve. I can't be concerning myself with relationship quirks right now.

Same day, just later.

Haha! I couldn't keep my big fat mouth shut! I gave myself away. I pretended to be bothered by a conversation he had with BM1 just to bring up BM2. I asked him if he had talked to her recently. He fucking said no! Then quickly, he said she emailed him to pick up her mail. I asked him if he was sure he didn't email her first. He denied emailing her first, made up a bunch of excuses as usual, and then talked circles around me. He is good with his words like that. Oh, well. I know the truth. Thank God. His mom asked if I was preggo, he denied it. She didn't believe him. She said that he could never ask her for help. Whatever. My mom and Ice's mom are not interested. I'm not mad. seven months till I see your face, my baby! Muah* Love, Mommy

I was hardly communicating with my mom or my dad. Ice and I lived in our own world, and while we had indeed started to tell family and friends we were pregnant, this turned out not to be something my mother was willing to bond with me over. She never got over losing her first son, and my being pregnant must have triggered some ugliness inside of her. She was shut down for this part of our time together. I didn't mind, Ice was enough for me at this point.

February 2, 2007

> *I'm at the South Central welfare office, with my bestie
> Wilona, applying for medical and food stamps. Ice is at
> home, I am still mad at him. I made him sleep on the couch
> last night. We had a long heated discussion about BM2. In
> circles. But, you know what, I actually don't care. I have
> someone else to worry about now. He is as big as a small
> strawberry. He already kicks his little nub legs to build mus-
> cle. My strong lil man. Mommy can't wait for the baby! I'm
> starving! Chocolate milk and chicken cup-o-noodles. Love
> always, Mommy.*

**Ice and I were struggling to find middle ground. I was
so young and jealous of his lifestyle, I often threw fits about
nothing. The pregnancy and its uncertainty thrust us into
a whirlwind of anxiety and darkness. Neither of us were
prepared. I was facing the thought of having to be a single
mother at 22, if things didn't work out. Was I really ready
for that?**

**We were drifting apart, and I couldn't decide between
being a mother and being in a relationship with him. I didn't
feel like I could have them both. Still we kept pushing for us.
We flew out to Hawaii for a show, and ended up staying longer, to try and rekindle our love and to make final decisions
about our baby on the way.**

February 18, 2007

> *Aloha from Hawaii! Again, we are still here. We are sup-
> posed to leave, like, yesterday. Whatever, we need more time
> I guess. Valentine's Day was great. We went snorkeling and
> saw everything, including turtles. A sign of love, according
> to the locals. I got a call about a job that I had applied for
> before we left. I got it, then quit three days into it. I am just*

a fuck up I guess. As of March 6th, I will be three months in. Leaving six months till I am due. How is this supposed to work? I need to make a decision quickly! I have a baby coming that I will have to support alone, or however Ice wants to help. I just need to be more prepared. Traveling is nice, I can't front on that. But it's his life, not mine. He's the "Star." I'm just BM3. I can't keep doing this to myself. I still don't have a phone, I am completely isolated from my friends and family. Ice is ALWAYS on his phone, "handling" business. I feel bad for him now. He has five women in his life who are somewhat dependent on him. I don't want… NO, I will never be one. Nor will my son be dependent. I found out that this is a special year for my son to be born. 2007, the year of the boar. However, every 600 years is the year of the Golden Boar. Well, my love, we are about to take off. I love you endlessly.

February 20, 2007

I shouldn't be here, ruining this man's life, his perfect existence. He hates me. There is no way around it. I do not have it figured out, and I'm not sure how we got here. We fight constantly, except right before, or during sex. We're not the friends we used to be. We behave more like "baby mama" and "baby daddy." He writes hate songs about me now. My biggest fear is coming true. He will put my existence out with his words. He is going to hate me the most. The pain I felt listening to his hate songs about me, while I am three months pregnant with his child, was completely unbearable. Every time we fight, it is my fault. My raging hormones have uncontrollably taken over my body and mind. He no longer understands me. We're drifting further and further apart. I don't make him happy anymore, as if I ever really did. He tells me that I can cry in front of him, then mocks me for doing so…? 20 years of solid pain, and now he is added to

my list of people who will never love me. I think I am just
unloveable. I need to face it.

I want to reflect a similar notion to this sentiment. I feel
it often, when I am brushing my elbows with love. I think
what happens is all the versions that we ever were, stay filed
inside us, like apples *versions* on *pages*. Sometimes, a man or
love interest will trigger something inside, and I can hear
this young 22 year old girl whisper in my ear, "you're just
unloveable." I become removed from my present self, and
tormented with a more ancient version of me.

The trick is to lean into it. Listen to that young girl, she
just wants to be heard. The words she's whispering, just need
to be said. It's nothing more than an old habit, but they mean
nothing to me now. Because now I know, I *am* love. It's impossible for you to not be loveable. A therapeutic step in my
forties, for the hurting and inexperienced 20-year-old me.
Lean into it. Allow these words to be said, and heard, and
let them float away like steam which has released its energy.
It's important I keep this girl alive, well dressed, well fed,
and loved. That's the thing about loving yourself, you must
love all of you.

Same day...

> *Ice and I just can't seem to get to the bottom of our troubles.*
> *They only began when I got pregnant. I'm confused, so is*
> *he. We're just not on the same page anymore. Yesterday he*
> *suggested that Tyler from the Chicken Coup be the godfather*
> *for our son. I jokingly said I didn't even want him to be the*
> *father. Yah, I probably shouldn't have said that. We fought*
> *and he left. Before he left, he said to me, "Sophia, the only*
> *reason you stay, is because you can't leave. You can't get a*
> *ticket to Merced, and you have no place to stay here." He is*
> *absolutely right. Unfortunately, before I came, I knew that*

was going to happen. But here is what he is wrong about, I stay because I want to. I love him, and I want this to work. I'm still pregnant and he is the father. Of course, I want this to work. I am forever indebted to him for giving me this gift of motherhood. He is my favorite person, no matter what. But being pregnant with his third child has driven me to insecurity and insanity. I see the difference in his face now when he looks at me. There is a loss of love, even if I try my hardest to please him, I will always go wrong. I have cried greatly in front of him, when I am at my most vulnerable, he says that's me. Walking out of the house tonight, he looks at me and says, I'm just like my mother. I won't let that bother me, even though he knows how much that could hurt, if I thought for a second he actually believed that. I did insult his ability to make the most of his money...NEVER TALK SHIT TO A MAN ABOUT HIS FUNDS. I deserved it. All this just makes me feel like we shouldn't have this baby. It's tearing us apart, instead of bringing us closer. Not that it works like that...but, goddamn. Why bring a child into this already fucked up world, when his own world crashed before he even arrived? I don't want an absent father for my child, nor do I want him to have a bitter mother. He deserves the best. Ice just can't give that to us right now. ★What a mess! Ten months deep, and this is where we are. SNW

February 25, 2007

Hey, you. Well, since the last time I talked to you, I have completely changed my life. Things between Ice and I heated and escalated so much. We keep blaming it on the hormones. But there was something else screaming out for help inside of me. I had to figure it out, we had to figure it out. I have the fight inside me, if you will, to resist becoming my mother. My battle against my inner self. Ice and I decided that we have enough faith in who and what we are to not have this child right now. Neither of us are prepared for this. So we're going to do the unusual, and not have this child. To save him and to save us from what no parent wants.

February 27, 2007

Today is the last day that I will get to be pregnant. My appointment is tomorrow morning, at 10:50 am. I am horrified. This pregnancy was nothing but a miracle, a blessing from God. We prayed for this baby. I am so disappointed in myself. I can't even complete my first pregnancy. Entirely pathetic. We figure though, if we're going to be together years from now, why not wait till the right time? I cannot make the drastic change from my current state to motherhood without his help. People are always saying that they are going to give their children what they never had. Well, I am no different. I want to provide my children with what I never had. A mother and a father, together, under one roof. A stable upbringing. This world is fucked up enough without my child having to wonder where his father is. I know who my father is, and he is one hell of a man. The best one I know, in fact, and I have got to give that to my child. Ice has what it takes to be a great father. But he is right smack-dab in the middle of a career change. He is about to put out his fourth solo album, and for him to stop and think about a third child? No way. If Ice really is the miracle man, then he can knock me up again. Maybe in three years or so. We have to build up to it. Create a strong foundation, on which we can support other members of our family. Including the three beautiful kids we currently have. If my baby could see his life ahead of him now, he might thank me. Ice is too good of a man/ father to have his son living away from him, because he and his mother do not get along. No one in this situation deserves that. What would happen if we were to have this child right now? Throwing away my miracle child is a cross I will carry alone. Ice can walk beside me in this disaster, but he will never understand the pain, suffering, and guilt I am about to face. Remembering my almost child for the rest of my life. I hope, because I can't even pray. I can't imagine how God could hate me, too. But I'm sure he can, if everyone else I love does. What I am doing is wrong, but it would be even more wrong to have the baby. Forgive me, Lord, for I am about to sin.

No Love, I'm sorry, strawberry baby, I hope you will understand.

My strawberry baby. I still do. It's the only hope I allowed myself to hold at the time, and one I cultivate to this day. I made a decision at that moment to give up hope on the possibility of motherhood for me at that time. I saw my mother, and the way she treated me, but couldn't separate myself from that image. I was paralyzed. This felt like the one thing in life that I wouldn't be able to handle. That I couldn't handle. So, I gave up on you, strawberry baby; gave up hope for a life with you. Despite the vacillation to come, I had already let you go.

February 28, 2007

9:53 am

Almost there…I am dreading my steps, my feet feel like cement. I have also been avoiding mirrors. I can't bear the sight of my own face. It disgusts me. I called a friend who has done this before to see what I am in for. It sounds no good. Ice is ok. He got too drunk last night, so unfortunately, he is in one of those moods. You know, the one where I can't talk to him. I wish he would cry with me. I need him the most.

10:43 am

We're here. There are more people in the waiting room than I would like to see.

11:14 am

They just made me pee.

11:21 am

I'm too scared to write right now, but I can't think of what else to do. I am in the prep room about to go for my ultrasound. It's really happening. I'm on the table with a hospital sheet covering my privates. I am about to see my strawberry baby one last time.

11:49 am

Well, that's over. I need to have a cigarette. I have been doing so good since I found out. But I need a cigarette, right now. I'm going to go find Ice. Baby- If I die. I loved you, and I am deeply sorry for the monster I have become. This is my last entry before I go under. I hope he sees the ultimate sacrifice I am giving for him. Love, Sophia N. Saber

They pulled me back to check my vitals. When the roller coaster clicks upwards, you know there is no going back... Except if they stop you in your tracks. They sent me back out to the waiting room. Given the opportunity to exit the ride, I did. I chickened out. When we went to go smoke a cigarette, we left. I couldn't do it. I wasn't ready.

March 5, 2007

> *I am here at Matty's studio in the Valley with Ice. He is recording a song for his album. The beat is probably the best beat I have ever heard in my life. No kidding. And my man is rapping on it. He is so good, he is super good at what he does. I'm just sitting on the couch writing to you as usual. Cameron just showed up to record, he's one of the guys from Oregon. This studio space is small, so I asked if I could go hang out with his girl around the corner, while the boys finished. I am still pregnant, having symptoms. I didn't want to be in a small room with four people, three of whom were working bodies. I was just taking up space. I told/asked Ice and he threw a lightweight bitch fit. He said the only reason I am here was so I could be with him in the studio. He likes me next to him while he is working. It's kind of endearing. I love spending time with him in the studio. It's one of the places we really shine. We are a great team. We seem to work well together in this environment. But I have no social life of my own, so when I get the opportunity, I try to jump on it. Anyway, we got in a really bad fight last night. He hit me so hard I was unconscious for a few minutes. I'm not totally innocent in the brawl, but he definitely went too far. He went so far that I should have decided to leave. You know, that thing that smart people do. Oh, yeah, learn from their mistakes…Nope, not me. I am still here, believing in painful love. The good in him outweighs the bad. I just hope that problem does not persist for very long. I sure would hate to think I only attract wife beaters and cheaters. Love Always, Sophia N. Saber*

Ice and I kept fighting, and the days were passing so slowly. Each moment with unclear intentions, would I throw up, overheat, or swing from my moods like apes in a tree. I was just exhausted by the whole thing. I knew deep down the right answer was to terminate the pregnancy. I was avoiding it, procrastinating. I knew it would not only affect my present, but that it had a severe potential to haunt me in my later years. The unknown was terrifying, not to mention the people holding picket signs and having opinions of what I should do with my body, and what it creates. Fuck them though, they mean nothing. They are only concerned with me, because being concerned with their own issues is much harder.

I pushed forward and did the hard thing. I got the abortion and it was not as physically painful as I thought. The recovery was non-linear, and the swift shift from pregnant to not pregnant, was also an unforeseen unpleasantry. However, emotionally, I felt a huge weight was lifted. I knew, this time I had done the right thing. To this day, almost twenty years later... I still stand by my side. It was the right choice for me, my baby, and Ice.

March 11, 2007

> *Hey, you. From now on, you will be talking to a totally different person, I have grown miles in the past few days. I got my abortion on March 7, 2007. The worst day of my life, by far. I felt horrible, the poison in my arm, the emptiness in my heart, and no more morning sickness. It has only been a few days, and I do not feel like a pregnant person anymore. I'm ok with the decision I made, I did the right thing. I know I hurt God, but he has my baby, for sure. I will see him someday, in heaven. I feel good knowing that if I don't get to have my son, God will have him. Pathetic, the things I trick myself to believe. Other than my abortion, I found out who I am. You know, this journey that I have been on to find me? Funny thing. I already am who I am. It's time for me to just accept me. I am not a model, singer, or actress. I just am who I am. The answer to who I am is me. A two letter word, so simple, so obvious. I have been overlooking*

*simplicity. I wanted to create and control, I wanted to rule.
Well, she did. Ice helped me to resurrect little Sophia. The
hurt and vulnerable me. The honest open minded me. She
cries from pain, and hides way down deep inside, and fears
love. He found her and loved her. Then there is the other
Sophia, she has an attitude worse than her mother. She is
ice cold. She built a wall around baby Sophia, and is often
mean to her. Keeping her locked up behind the wall she built.
She soaks up all baby Sophia's nourishment, and spits it out
as poison, Big Sophia hates that she is impulsive, rude, and
most of all, selfish. I also see her way more often. When I
look in the mirror. There are so many sides to me…which
one is me?!*

*Rest in peace, strawberry baby 3.7.07 Mommy loves you,
and I will always remember my first.*

Ice left me for about three days to do a show in Oregon.
I stayed back, due to my need to be alone for a few days, and
to heal from the operation. I kept his phone to be in touch,
and to ensure I wasn't in the hood with no communication.
However, BM1 called, and I answered. She asked if I was,
"ok," and she told me that Ice had told her everything. I
didn't show her my true reaction. I was shocked and devastated, placing my hand over my mouth and nose while I
sobbed uncontrollably. I realized right then, that while I was
in the operating room, Ice was telling her exactly what was
going on. She was inquiring about something, and instead of
saying he didn't have it, he told her where he was and what
was going on. He claimed that I had told him I couldn't have
kids. BM1 and I had a great conversation, what a woman I
thought. I liked her, I really did. She felt bad. I felt worse.

When I confronted him, I had intentions on leaving him.
This was the worst thing he could have done, never in a mil-
lion years had I imagined he could be so cruel. He was upset

that I answered the phone. He was upset that I met the truth. Instead of hashing it out like a couple of grown ups, we did rails of coke and had a heart to heart. Ice, I said, I need to know the truth about everything right now. Let's start clean. What else have you done? He said that he had a conversation with BM2 about me in which he called me crazy and a loser. I did not like what I was hearing, but he was not wrong. I had so much work to do on myself, I couldn't even argue. I felt satisfied with his honesty, and we both agreed a reset was manageable.

May 26, 2004

> *Hi, sorry, so sorry, I have been away for so long. So much has happened. First off, I miss my nieces. I miss the hell out of them. I love those girls like there is no tomorrow. Everything between Ice and I is good once again. Order has been restored, and things are only getting better. We are still babies in our relationship. We are still learning from each other. We celebrated our one-year anniversary on May 10th. My, how time flies. Feels as though we have been together for centuries! He is my forever, and it feels good to know that, finally. We have so many years to go. He sees me for the dirty little me that I am. I see him for the dirty little him that he is. Neither of us are angels, this is why we connect so well. As for me, I am finally growing into my skin. I am who I never thought I would be. A mean girl. Who saw that coming?! I don't put up with anybody's shit, nor do I put my shit on anybody else. I'm not exactly sure who I thought I was going to be, but I am going to embrace it. Whether I fit in or not. I don't care what people say, if they don't like me, oh well. I don't give a fuck. My father loves me, and so does Ice. Speaking of my father, I am making a grave mistake by not being with the one man whom I know will love me forever, 100%... My hero, my mentor, my best friend.*

He is 57. We seldom have sprinkled phone calls. None of it is going to matter much when I am crying over his death. Regretting not spending more time with the one man I do love, and that loves me back. While we are on the subject, my mother is back. She calls me and I call her. She is also on myspace. I am trying to not let her die without knowing me first. And, before she dies, I want to make sure she is loved and knows it. I want her to love me and I want to know it. I know she can. I miss my little brother. He is growing up, just like me. We have gone separate ways but are still meeting in the middle. We are cut from the same cloth, no matter how far apart we are——- we are one in the same. I still hope I can reach him, before life kicks the shit out of him. I've been writing a lot. Just not here. In my pink notebook. Raps, poetry, dope shit. I just can't materialize it. I can't be vocal...I don't get it!? WTF is wrong with me?! I'm scared. It's so uncomfortable for me to use my voice. Why?! Love Always, Sophia N. Saber

June 19, 2007

We live in separate worlds, under one roof. He will never understand me. My pain, my dreams. And I will never understand him. I'm a fool, a complete fool. I live for him. Why? I no longer exist. I can't explain that very well. Later, SNS

June 21, 2007

A week ago, I had to be hospitalized. We were having sex, he came inside me, and 20 minutes later my lower abdomen exploded. The ambulance was called, I was in the worst pain of my life. He was by my side the whole time. I have ovarian cysts and he ruptured one. Not a good feeling. Also, it's a permanent condition. I will need to be careful in future sexual endeavors. Love Always, Sophia N. Saber

June something, 2007

> *Hi. I haven't been doing so well lately. Ice and I have changed for the worst. I'm losing my man. More likely, he is losing interest in me. He's got his eye on a new prize. Money and fame. He wants it so bad, he is spelling it out in his mashed potatoes. Not literally, but you know what I mean. He has broken up with me twice, I talked him out of it both times. A part of him realizes I am not worth having around. Once he got past the beauty and pussy, dissected my psyche, childhood problems, turned me inside out, rescued me from my Merced life, redressed me, showed me a whole new world, and taught me a new language... He is content and needs nothing more from me. He has totally consumed me, and now that I have nothing left to give, he is ready to leave.. I have no child to tie me to him. So, I lost twice. I haven't talked to my sister in days, nor anybody else, for that matter. I am scared for my future. He said he feels like a sucker for making the changes he has for me. He says, I stay with him because I have no other options. He says, without him I wouldn't exist. That I will never leave this country or be anybody of great importance like him! I love Ice. He knows me better than I know myself. I know him, too, and if I want to keep him forever, I have to let him go. Give him a break, and let myself grow a bit. Give him a chance to not just miss me, but miss us. He is important to my heart, my person, my humanity. But certainly not my survival. It is going to be so hard to face the day of saying goodbye to the one I spend every waking second next to. But, if I leave now, before he hates me, we will survive.*

Unfortunately, or fortunately, Ice and I stayed together for *two* more years. Two long years of raising a couple of pitbulls, and finding ways to renew and try again. We replaced our lost child with a family dog. When we lost our puppy, Bruce,

we took the loss harder than the abortion. We knew Bruce, he had toured with us and made appearances in magazines. We had been feeding him and taking care of him like he was our kid for close to a year when he had passed. He was our boy. When we lost him, we quickly replaced him with a boy puppy from his own litter.

While Ice was ready to move on, I was not. The failure of our attempt to grow a family kept repeating itself, and we began to fail each other. The drugs had continued, and I wasn't evolving the way I thought I should. We ended our time in July of 2009. I had stopped writing in my diary. I had taped a picture of my sonogram into my last strawberry baby page, so, every time I opened the book I found myself being cruelly reminded of the pain I had endured. I kept telling myself that I needed more time to get over it.

The thing about us, and about these entries, is that when I write, I do it to vent. I write to maintain balance in my psyche. I didn't write when he was sweet, or sane, or when things were working in a well-balanced manner. We were, if anything, good friends. To this day, we are very cordial with one another. Towards the end of us, I had stopped going everywhere with him and began to model somewhat seriously. I had a few stable gigs, and I was making my own connections with people. I did not love it, though. I just felt like, at that time, my options for economic success were limited to vocalist, dj, model, or actress.

Often, when Ice and I stayed up on coke for nights on end, we would write together. He would constantly work with me to develop any musical talent I may have been hiding inside. He was a great teacher: kind, patient, albeit, a bit of a liar when he would tell me "good work." I think he believed it. He believed in me. Also, his dream was to travel and work with his woman. This is why I was his merch girl. He had expressed to me that he wanted me to be his back up vocalist, so we would play pretend shows in the living room for a full house of dogs and cocaine rails. We really did make the most of our time together while we could.

Along with throwing epic shows in our living room, I cooked the best I could for him, as often as I could, and we would watch TV. We loved South Park, CSI, and documentaries. We watched a documentary called Zeitgeist the last year we were together. The documentary was hosted by George Carlin, you know the one I'm talking about. It ties up the major religions in a singular story, told by the stars. This connection changed me overnight.

Before Ice and I broke up, God and I broke up. I've never experienced a more painful falling out. My religion was what I had thought rooted me to my soul. It was what had blanketed me in my youth, and is what brought me closer to my mother. Losing God meant that I was losing the most stable quality built into my foundation. Having a god grounded me, sheltered me, protected me from earthly entanglements and daily strife. Who was I without a god? This was the much bigger question beginning to brew.

CHAPTER 9

90210

Postal ZIP code for a fancy ass area in LA

August 2, 2009

*HAPPY BIRTHDAY, ICE! We talked last night.
I texted him around midnight, to say happy birthday.
We discussed our break up for the first time since it
happened. It went really well, and I am excited about
our future as friends and ex-lovers. I was angry, I
didn't get what I wanted from him, which was to become a mother. However, as the years pass by, my
patience and understanding grow. I know more about
what it is going to take, and I am finally ready to wait
for it. I don't look at our situation in a bad way. We
loved each other very much. And in the end it was not
hate that tore us apart, rather, silly amenities of this
technological world we live in. We are just two different
people who want two different things out of life. There
is nothing wrong with that. Happy birthday old, forever lost, love. Always,* **Sophia N. Saber**

August 7, 2009

*Hey, my love. I feel change coming. Big change. I have
goosebumps. The transition I am about to go through
will be major. Cane and Darcy are going to be very*

important people in my lifetime. Change is coming.
Not like Obama change, actual change. A little bit
of political humor for you there. Anyway, I feel like
good things are beginning to happen to me. Incredible
things. Things I have been waiting for my whole life.
25 is my time to shine! I have got what it takes to get
what I want, and what I want is wanting me back. I
need to let it love me. I need to accept the good, forget
the bad, and learn to let go. Darcy is my spice. I can
tell I am going to learn so much from her. I love her
daughter, she is such a special kid. Change is coming!
Love Always, **Sophia N. Saber**

I was finally on my own. I didn't have much, or make a lot of money. I wasn't even very comfortable where I was. But I had food, water, shelter, and I still had all of my shoes. I was content and safe, and at that point, that's all that mattered. I was working on getting over Ice, crying into late hours of the night. During the day, I was rebounding with a classmate from my new school.

I had enrolled at Abrams Technical College in downtown LA. I decided I was going to switch from modeling to mechanics. So, I signed myself up for a smog check six-month course, to begin my journey toward becoming an ACE certified mechanic.

On top of that, I was owning my social life, and I could feel that my skin was stretching over my new found persona. I was going out at night with my bestie, Weezy. A former girlfriend of one of Ice's band members. She and I had formed an intense bond over the period of time I was with him. We left our men at the same time, as well. Our paths were aligned. I was standing on my own, the way Ice said I couldn't.

A good mutual friend of mine and Ice's, Topiq, was in town for one of his shows. He was a musician from Colorado, where we had met him after a show at the fox, one evening. He called me and asked if I wanted to go see him perform in Malibu. I welcomed the invitation.

I wasn't sure who was going to be there. So, I put on a black wig and an odd dress, called myself Isabelle, and hit the road. Going to Malibu to drink and be merry. Once I had arrived, I was introduced to Topiq's sister, Athena. She lived in Silver lake, she was beautiful. Tall and goddess-like, with blonde hair and a perfect porcelain face, like that of an expensive french doll. She laughed easily, and walked with an unmatched confidence. She was studying to become an artist, though she already was one.

We talked into the early morning hours, laughing, sharing, drinking, and becoming instant friends. She asked if she could draw me sometime. I jumped at the idea.

"Of course! When?"

"Within the next three days? I'm not that busy now."

"OK, I will see you tomorrow evening around 7:00 pm?" It was a date.

The next day, I had a photoshoot, then I would go to her place. I was still a bit dolled up from make-up and costume, so, it would make for perfect drawing exposure. It felt a bit like the scene from Titanic, except I wasn't naked, and she wasn't Leonardo DiCaprio. She was better. It was definitely at that moment I knew, I liked her for more than just a friend. I didn't push it, due to my still existent confusion. We spent so much time together, I could almost say I lived with her. I was facing the same road blocks with Athena that I had faced with Mariah. When it comes down to it, I am not a lesbian. The way these certain women make me feel remains a great mystery.

I did however, live with my very dear friends, Cane and Darcy, in Beverly Hills. They had a multi-million dollar home. I was happy, I had good friends, and a bright light at the end of my tunnel. Not to mention, Ice and I had made amends. I had the green light I needed to finally move forward.

Athena's older brother, Eros and younger brother, Topiq had come to visit her. The four of us went to Disneyland together, and the day brought Eros and I very close. We talked, laughed, and played. The juvenile connection proved to be love at first sight. Eros and I wasted no time having serious feelings for each other, and continued our journey of romance for about two months. He lived in Florida, and for us, the long distance was more of a burden than anything. We called it quits, and remained very good friends.

Athena and I continued our pseudo-lesbian affair after Eros and I had parted. We flew to San Francisco to see an ex-lover of hers, and this brought us closer. We traveled well together. We understood one another, and I felt jealous seeing her with another man.

On the Virgin flight from LA to SFO, I asked her to be my girl-friend. She declined. She said that she wasn't looking for a relation-ship. I completely understood. I also wasn't looking. I was still testing out my wants and needs, and seeing what fit and what didn't. It had little effect on our actual connection.

School was going well, and I was still living in cushy Beverly Hills. My social life was finally becoming vibrant, and I was making real progress toward my future. We had a small break from school for Labor Day, so I left LA for Merced. I needed some time with my sister and the girls, and to see Daniel so I could catch up on all the happenings.

August 28, 2009

> *Hey, you! So I am in Merced. Been here for about a week now. Basically just to be with the girls, also I missed Daniel. I am staying with him. We talk on the phone almost everyday. Since I broke up with Ice, he has really had my back for strength and support. Also, Ali is here. The three of us are just chilling, smoking blunts, and playing the new Madden. Whatever that means. It feels just like the good old days. Our divorce will be finalized in thirty days, and I will finally be Miss. Saber again. Never again will I drop my name. I will always be a Saber. Anthony moved to San Francisco, he's a chef now. I miss him, as well. My mother lives in Phoenix with her fourth husband.*

*I still talk to her every now and then. I'm still getting
her used to the idea of just loving me for who I am, and
not who she wanted me to be. I feel so bad her mother
never loved her at all, she claims. Anyway, I'm going
to go pick up my eldest niece from school and surprise
her. I'll talk to you later.*

Love Always, Sophia Nahlah Saber

After my break, I went back home to 90210 and continued school
as usual; school, home, and picking up all the pieces. It was all coming
together, but still very fragile. I was finally regulating my relationship
with my mother. We had sparse contact, but when we did, it was
usually amicable. My father's presence in my life had also dwindled,
but was still loving. This was the first time I was really on my own
since I had emancipated myself at 15.

I felt like I had finally begun to balance all the spinning plates.
Meanwhile, that change I kept visualizing and demanding be of ser-
vice to me was creeping in. Little did I know, that change would be
at the heart of what would alter me forever. As per usual, after school
one day I was calling to talk to Daniel to tell him about a boy I had
met, and also to coordinate thanksgiving.

I couldn't get a hold of him. I called my sister and told her I
couldn't reach him. I had a sick feeling in my gut. She told me I
was being dramatic, but I asked her to call around anyway. She got
nothing, no response. We figured he was out. Three hours later, she
called me crying, "Sophia, you were right. Daniel is dead." I couldn't
believe the words out of her mouth. Would she actually joke around
about something like that? How could this be?! No. It's not true.

She insisted and was sobbing herself, so I realized it was not a joke.
My vision blackened and began to tunnel. I fainted down a thirty step
staircase in my mini-mansion residence. A bit of time had passed, I
must have been out for a few minutes or so. When I came too, my
legs were numb, and I had an excruciating pain in the side of my face.
It was all miniscule compared to the emotional pain I was feeling. I

couldn't help the theatrics I was displaying. I couldn't see beyond the rivers flowing from my eyes. My phone was in pieces at the bottom of the stairs, well beyond my reach. Was this all a dream?

No, this was not a dream. That game of Madden would be the last time I ever saw my dear friend Daniel. I found the house phone and called my sister back. She explained the situation, as told to her by his cousin. On October 17th, 2009, he was murdered. A bullet wound to the back of the head. In his sleep.

My best friend, mentor, and older brother was dead. Brutally murdered. I was beyond stunned, I was in shock. I called Cane and Darcy in a hysterical manner. They rushed home, and then proceeded to drive me four hours up north to be with my family and friends in this time of unprecedented crisis.

I stayed in Merced, cuddled with my ex-husband, Anthony, and all of our other friends who loved and cherished Daniel. We were all suffering a major loss. The funeral was a huge event. Hundreds of people came to give their respects. Daniel had touched a lot of people in his short time on earth, I was very fortunate to be one.

December 14, 2009

Hello, my friend. It would seem as though a new girl is coming to replace who I am. Change came, you know that change that I felt so strongly? Daniel was killed. Daniel was my foundation for my adult life decisions. Every decision I have ever made was first run by him, since I was 15 years old! He was my constant soul. The soul that was going to start the walk with me and finish the race with me. He was my strength. He was THE most irreplaceable person I have ever met. Nobody would ever, could ever replace my very near and dear friend. He was my chosen brother. It's taken me so long to write this to you. Writing is so difficult for me now. All I have to offer in words is pain and sorrow...one event after the next, since 2006. Since his murder, I have been in a constant state of numbness. I walk around each day in a silent blur. The sun, the moon, doesn't matter, I have completely lost myself. The Sophia Nahlah Saber that I was born as, no longer exists. Masterfully murdered by me. The new me. Numb me. Today, I would be a mother to a three year old. Fuck me. **Sophia N Saber**

In order to cope with the pain I felt, I turned to a familiar face, an old comfort with a new name. Morphine. I had moved out of my plushy estate with people who love me, to be in darkness, to be alone, and to be numb. I couldn't smile, or laugh, or think. I used money from government loans to buy my drugs, until I dropped out of school. After which, I flipped food stamp benefits, dealing with local crackheads and plugs who made house calls to various crack dens. I spent my days sleeping and my nights sedated. Lying around in shaded rooms with other people, drowning out the noise of our lives. I returned to a state of pseudo-elation. I had found escape, yet again, provided by drugs. I traded weed and cocaine for the downers I truly wanted; I was killing myself slowly. The pain of loss I had endured up till this point was too much for my tiny sleepy soul.

Everyone began to worry about me, including Ice. He was checking in on me and making sure that I was alive. He didn't like where I was living and how things were looking for me. He was in contact with my mother, and together they urged me to seek help by moving out of LA. I was hesitant and careless about my status. This continued through November, and by December, I bit the bullet and asked my father if I could come home.

I always felt I had more of a home with him than with my mother. She was understanding of what I was going through. She had welcomed me to join her in Phoenix for safety and rehabilitation, though she would expect me to turn to God, and I just couldn't agree to that. God and I had broken up, and I was determined to never go back, even though I still wasn't sure how to move forward.

On Dec 26th, 2009, I made the move back to Colorado to heal

and to come off drugs. My father knew I was an addict. He knew that it was from Daniel's death, and he welcomed me home with empathetic open arms. Change sure had come. I was in pain and back in a foreign, unwelcoming place. All the recent progress I had made in California was wiped clean upon my arrival. I had to start back at square one. I had to meet myself in Colorado as a recovering addict, and as a grieving lost soul.

CHAPTER 10

A Quick Bite

Noun: a thing done or made quickly or hastily, in particular.

The Co-Worker

It's cold outside, very cold. I've made the transition back to Colorado, and this time it looks as though I am here for a while. I am in need of rehabilitation, love, and rest. I need to get my life together. My father let me revive myself for almost seventy-two days. I rested, shivered, and sweat in the darkness of my childhood home basement, alone. I'm not even sure he was aware of what I was going through.

By January, I had a job at Jiffy Lube in Louisville. I figured I could make that work. I hadn't finished school but I had learned enough to hold a position at the Mcdonalds of oil changes. The hiring manager was Chris, my seventh grade boyfriend, who cheated on me. I didn't recognize him at first, and even though he knew exactly who I was, he still hired me. After a day or two, I realized who he was, and in an instant all those feelings of adolescent excitement returned. Then the anger. He apologized, said he was young and stupid, and suggested we be friends since he was now my boss. We made it work.

Chris was still as charismatic as ever. There was a reason he was the boss. He became a salesman. The funny guy, the one everyone liked, was now slinging oil changes in the same town we attended junior high together, close to our ditch behind 7/11.

Then there was Nick, he was the floor manager. The one who whipped employees into shape, you either liked him or you didn't.

A bit of an asshole, but I liked him like that. We almost immediately fell into one another, his crass nature reminded me of D, so I gravitated toward him. He was a father to a son. Of which, I was wary; but he had introduced me to his son's mom, and I knew for sure she and he were a thing of the past. I tried my hardest to coerce him into having a relationship with me. But alas, he was still in love with his most recent.

I had started sleeping with him for healing, I thought I wanted love from him, or from that relationship. I didn't. I just wanted to feel good somewhere in my life. I thought Daniel would like him, that they would get along, and that was also calming for me. We worked on cars together, there is nothing sexier than a man all greased up and dirty. I swear, there isn't. He had my undivided attention. The sex was amazing. It was rough, and a bit dirty. He knew how to put me in a choke hold and give it to me like a rock star.

However, I always felt empty afterwards. This was the first time I had ever paid attention to this particular emptiness. I was becoming more aware of the pattern or, dare I say, addiction. It had been setting in since I had lost my virginity. I had always turned to sex to balance the pain I was feeling.

Nick and I only lasted three months. Then he told me he needed to get *her* back, that he had his fun, but that their paths were what he had wanted, *she* was what he wanted.

So, he let me go.

The Ginger

After Nick, I went through men like I was scarfing bacon for breakfast. I was transitioning from being in a relationship since I was 15, to being single and a full grown adult. I was still experimenting with myself, testing out all my body parts, and stretching my mind. My sexuality always sat at the forefront of exploration. I was in a new environment, mom-free, god-free, boyfriend-free, husband-free. I wanted to see what was outside the palace walls, so I took a stroll, and found the Ginger who kicked everything off.

Athena had come out to visit. We were on Pearl Street, a pedi-mall turned strip bar after sundown; We were all in good spirits, eating, laughing, and joking around on a bench outside a favorite dance club of mine called, "Round Midnight." The only place a girl could dance on table tops. Once we were all sweaty, and had run down our dancing batteries, we went outside and ordered gyros. We were wasted. Colorado elevation wasted.

He was sitting directly across from me. The ginger. Without a second thought, I put my sandwich down, crawled across the table in front of six people all sitting across from one another, grabbed him by his collar, and began to kiss his face. I'm not even sure I had completely chewed or swallowed my bite. That didn't bother this ginger, or me. I do remember a few friends protesting the aggressive PDA, but only because we didn't all have phones and public digital spaces to post such tom-foolery.

Reckless making out in a public space had commenced. Athena soon stopped the ridiculousness, redirected my behavior, and kept the pearl street shenanigans moving forward. We finally retired back to her friend's house. We played board games, drinking games, and games I didn't want to be playing. At least, not while there was a trampoline out back staring me down.

I responded to its call. I stripped my clothing off, down to my panties and bra, grabbed Mr. Ginger, and off we went. The next thing I remember is the morning light beginning to kiss my face and wake me from my sleep. I felt the instability under my body very quickly and woke up in a panic. I was on a trampoline. My panties were around my ankles, and there was someone next to me.

I rolled over to see who was holding me. I moved my hair from my face to see his red hair covering his face.

"Oh, you're a ginger." I said playfully, but in surprise.

He giggled, "Good morning to you as well."

I pulled my panties up from my ankles, and hopped on my way.

Never to see this fine young man, who catered to a broken girl's sexual desires one drunken night on pearl, again.

The Comedian

By now, it is late March or early April of 2010. I have been clean for nearly five months, holding down my lubrication position at Jiffy Lube, and *still* learning to be an adult. My father, brother, and myself are enjoying our time being the three of us again. The way we used to be when I was young and we lived in Boulder. We get along just fine, but like any crew, we have our differences.

One night, My father asks us if we want to go have a laugh."There is a comedy club down in Westminster, and I have free tickets for doing some sound work a few weeks back. Would you two knuckleheads like to go?" My brother responds first,

"Will there be alcohol?"

"Yes," My father says in disdain.

"Well, is it free?" My brother adds.

"Yes," My father annoyingly agrees.

"Ok, I'm in."

Then there's my line of questioning:

"Will there be boys?" My father drops his head.

"My two children and their vices. Yes, Sophia. I'm sure there will be boys."

"Ok, I'm in." With that we were off.

We entered the venue, and immediately I felt as though I was at work. I should be carrying Ice's sound equipment, setting up my merch booth over there in that corner where the comedians were selling CD's before the show. I was saddened by the thought of what I had recently lost and was brought back to many sweet memories.

Nevertheless, I ordered my tequila, and sat down next to my boys. The show started and we laughed our way through each set. Every comedian was funnier than the last. Finally our headliner got up on stage and I almost peed my pants. He had us laughing so hard. His jokes were aimed at his own unhappiness with life, as most comic's jokes are. *I'm fat and old and my penis doesn't work.* It's a bittersweet relationship these men must have with themselves.

After the show, my father and brother were busy fussing with the technology of the show, and I was left to find trouble. I had never known myself to be attracted to tall, thin, bald, and hysterical, but on this day I was. I meandered my way over to where he was, and stood right in his eyesight. He called me over, opened up the gate behind the merch stand, and kept me there while he sold CDs and signed autographs. When no one was wanting his attention, he was focused on me. I was right at home.

He continued to make me laugh. I love to laugh. It turns out laughter felt almost as good as sex did. So, we exchanged numbers and my father came to retrieve me. Of course, he had no trouble knowing exactly where I was. Of course, I was with the headliner. Of course, I was behind the rope.

The next day he would call and we would talk. There was laughter and plenty more sarcasm, but even more enticement. He explained that he was staying with a friend for a few weeks in the town a few miles from my home. If I could get to him, we could hang out. So I asked my father for a ride.

My poor father. I wanted that boy, and I was determined to find my way in the snow—"Don't cock block, dad! For fuck's sake. Don't you want me gone for a bit?" Finally he gave in and drove me to be with Mr. Comedian. We spent the day watching old black and white films, in front of some fire and snowfall. Once we couldn't handle just kissing, we drove to play pool in my neck of the woods and to spend some time at my house. We soon found ourselves naked in one another's presence. I kept on my knee high socks, he also kept his on. We had sex and kept each other laughing.

We hung out a little for the following weeks, sex or no sex, we liked each other. I, of course, fantasized about marriage, but I'm sure he only fantasized about my socks and what was between the legs that wore them. Either way we kept each other amused for three months or so. Meeting in California and Colorado.

Until one day he explained that the long distance was driving him nuts, he didn't think he was ever going to be the man I needed him to be. It was best we go our separate ways.

So, he let me go.

CHAPTER 11

Fourth Of July

|*AKA*| *My Favorite Holiday*

I was a bit heart broken, and unwelcoming of the new pattern I saw beginning to form in my life. Nick and I were not getting along well at work, so I quit working at Jiffy Lube and applied at Grease Monkey. I was hired and set to make the official switch in July, to put in a proper two weeks notice. For now, it was mid-June, 2010. I started planning a small vacation in between jobs. I would travel back to California for the fourth of July to see my nieces. My sister and I planned a trip to San Francisco to watch the fireworks on the pier, and to spend some time with Anthony. He was now a big shot chef living in the city.

My final two weeks couldn't end soon enough. I packed my bags and off I went. It was a much deserved break from working life, rehabilitation for half the year, and re-adjusting to life at home as an adult with my father and brother. It would be a busy vacation back home with my sister and the girls.

I arrived on July second, and met the girls in Merced at the train station from the airport. We went back to my sister's place and had a nice family dinner. The next day we ventured to the city from Merced, and ate at the museum where Anthony was the head chef. We were spoiled that day. Soon after our meal and a long walk around the park, we returned to his place completely pooped. We slept like babies.

In the morning, I woke to my phone ringing incessantly. Someone was trying very urgently to get a hold of me. It was my father. Strange, he never calls me, I thought. Not even at home. So, I answered in a bit of a sleepy haze.

"Hello, Papa."

"Sophia, your mother is dead." A long pause. I needed to wake up a bit. Maybe I was dreaming.

"I'm sorry, what did you say?"

"Your mother, she is dead. She died this morning in her sleep."

"NO! What? NO!" I dropped the phone and ran outside as far as I could and collapsed. Screaming at the top of my lungs. My sister ran after me, she had picked up the phone after I had dropped it. My father repeated himself to her, and she held me while I wept wildly. I was crying and shaking uncontrollably. I had just spoken to my mother three days before. We had been fighting about a post on Facebook. She was trying to get me to return to God in my recovery, and I was refusing. She was dead, and we were at odds.

The girls woke up to the crying coming from their mother and aunt, and without knowing what was wrong, they joined in the huddle of their elders and began to weep, as well. The wailing carried into the streets, and neighbors were watching. I didn't see them, though. I didn't see anything. I, too, was dead.

I scraped myself off the cement and limped back into the house. We walked/huddled our way back in. I sat in complete silence with my sister and the girls. I called my little brother, and we sat on the phone in silence and tears, ending our childhood.

I hung up the phone with my brother, took a long hot shower, and decided that this couldn't ruin my time with my nieces. After all, they were still here now, and I needed to cherish my time with them. I held my nieces and explained that in the night, my mother went to heaven while she slept. The truth was, she had gone in to have a surgery done on her nose for sleep apnea correction. She made it through the surgery fine, but her heart stopped at some point in the night. She was at home, on pain meds. She was sleeping comfortably in her favorite place, her bed.

She spent a lot of time in bed, from what I can remember as a child. Always reading in bed, or praying. When I was really young, she would smoke cigarettes and read trash magazines, on her bed. In these moments, I remembered everything I could about her, and then forgot it all. This process repeated all day, week, month, and year...till now. Our mother was dead. I felt the weight of the world instantly placed on my shoulders. My life's purpose had come about through her death. The person I was here to replace was gone, and now I had to fill her shoes. I wasn't ready.

I remember that day, clear as crystal. Time was going by so slow, my every move was ingrained into the gray matter of my brain. I dressed, slowly. I wore red, white, and blue. Tears fell. I did the older one's hair, she was less fussy. The tears dried. We were silent. My sister rubbed my back, the tears fell, again. I folded into a ball, one last shiver before we were in public. I folded and collapsed into myself. The tears poured, my voice roared, my body trembled with enough force to move the earth. We sat in silence some more. They were patient. They suffered with me.

I stood up, the younger one grabbed my hand and said, "I love you." The older one grabbed my waist, "You will always have us." My sister brought us all in together. We hugged, and left. My sister called Anthony and let him know what happened. He demanded we go to the museum right away. He took me in his arms and kissed me gently, he held me in silence while I cried for a bit.

"I'm not going to her funeral" I protested earnestly.

"Fuck her for dying on the fourth of July. Fuck her for leaving me again! Without saying goodbye, or I love you. She never told me she loved me. I never really told her I loved her."

"Sophia, your mother loved you. She just had her own way of showing it."

"How am I ever supposed to love? How can I ever love, if my mother never showed me she loved me. Fuck her, Anthony. Just like her to ruin my favorite holiday."

He knew I needed to be angry with her. I needed that anger to get me through my days and nights, till I could accept her. Accept us and forgive her. It was only hurting me. He let me be angry, and reminded me not to show the girls my anger. He kissed me once more on my forehead and sent me out with my family to celebrate American independence.

We walked the wharf in very forced spirits. The girls could read that I was in no state of mind to play or joke with them, I may as well have been a ghost. But, I smiled and tried my hardest to make my way through the crowds, without bursting at the seams. My mother is dead, my mother is dead, my mother is dead, kept repeating itself. For hours, days, weeks, this was all I could hear.

My father called me with funeral information a day or two later. I told him that I was declining the ceremony. I had just attended my best friend's funeral, and I refused to attend my mother's. I explained that funerals were for the living and not for the dead. How fake everything was and what stupid ceremonies humans have for dead bodies. I didn't care about her body. I didn't care to see her lifeless flesh just lying there.

He pleaded with me. He told me that if I didn't go, for the rest of my life, I would regret not closing the deal. I could never go back and say goodbye. I told him, I would have to learn to say goodbye on my own terms. He knew he wasn't going to win this battle, so he had my brother call me.

"Sister." He said calmly in this voice he only uses when he wants something.

"I need you there." I needed him, too. We are cut from the same cloth, him and I. So, I had my flight booked the next day and was off to Phoenix, for what I hoped was the last time in my life.

I met him and my cousin, Victoria, who had become a second daughter to my mother. My mother was the best thing that happened to my little sister/cousin. Without her, Victoria would have also grown up loveless. It was through the connection Victoria had with my mother that I learned she did have it in her to love a young girl the way a mother should. Through their connection, I felt my mothers love, and right then and there, I was able to forgive her. I knew she loved me.

My brother had also been fighting with my mother for the past year. He finally came to terms with who he thought she really was. The two of them barely spoke. To him, her death was also tragic. She died missing the two children she knew, and the one she had given up for adoption at seventeen. Tragedy is an understatement. She died alone.

We flew home two days after the funeral, after extra time with the family and some proper goodbyes. I started my new job on July 11, 2010. My boss was more than understanding. He was so kind and sympathetic. He had lost his father in recent years, so we bonded over our loss. I worked hard from sun up till sun down. I became operations manager at the lube shop in no time. My skills were developing on the professional front, and so was my bank account. I was finally becoming a woman and taking care of myself. I was in mourning, yes, but in *her* absence I began to know myself.

In October of 2010, I decided I wanted to see the world. I felt I must. I suddenly knew how fast life could be stripped from you. I felt an urgent need to do the things I would do if I knew I was dying at some predetermined time. I planned a trip to Europe. I still hadn't left the country since Ice took me to Denmark. I really didn't know how or why I would go to Europe, but suddenly there was an *in*.

Athena had moved to Paris to attend art school, and invited me to come stay a while. I gladly did. I left in January 2011. I spent three days with my sister and the girls in California, then the remainder of the month in Paris with Athena. I turned 26 that year, on top of the Eiffel tower, standing next to Athena. We shared a kiss, and locked hands. It was the most romantic Parisian birthday a girl could wish for.

I spent some time in Belgium and the Netherlands, to meet with my dear friend, Peter. I met him on Venice beach in California a few years prior. We had built some feelings and explored them, as well. My time with him and in Amsterdam was nothing short of amazing! This was the first time I had really gotten a chance to explore Europe.

I took trains, and subways, smoked pot in public, and watched girls in red light windows. I was totally amazed.

It was like I was meeting America's parents. Everything was smaller and neater, people dressed differently, and spoke completely different languages in different countries as you quickly crossed borders. I really enjoyed myself, and traveling. Though, this was only partly what I had meant when I said see the world. I had other plans, but felt I needed to first warm-up. I was not yet a seasoned traveler, not yet ready for the underdeveloped world. Or was I?

Coming back from Europe gave me this deep sense of pleasure in myself, like I had accomplished some impossible task. I had found my passion. This sense of wonder and relief felt as though it could take the place of some of the more unhealthy vices I had been leaning on. Learning new ways and meeting new cultures felt right.

While there may have been a second coming, another tragic robbery of life, this time I was left with something. It was as though my mother gave me passion for traveling as a departing gift. It felt right, and I wanted much more of this feeling. So, I began to let her go…

CHAPTER 12

Mombasa, Kenya

noun: The most beautiful place on earth.

Then, there was Africa. I have had such a strong calling to this place since I was young. Very young. When assigned projects in my geography classes, I always chose Africa. I remember drawing the whole continent once, back when the DRC was called Zaire. I was fascinated by the language, the people, and culture. It went beyond interest. My whole life, something called me to this place.

I searched for months, thinking of ways to go. I felt urgency in the calling. Now is the time, I thought. Now is the time. I needed exposure to life. I felt a multitude of lessons just waiting for me to learn them. I felt closure with trouble's I had previously experienced. I felt growth, I felt truth. I spent what felt like years searching for the perfect opportunity. I wasn't even sure what I was looking for. I had never done something like this before.

Finally, a few weeks into my relentless search, I found an organization called "Children's Hope House." It was a Christian based organization. However, it was not, "I will give you water if you believe in my God," type of scenario. I went as a proud atheist. Lending my hand and heart to over 200 children, 50% of which were HIV positive. I wanted to go as a volunteer, and stay for two months. I needed space to heal. I explained to my boss that if I could take three months off, when I returned I would work my ass off for the next year. He not only agreed, but sponsored the trip. He paid for my ticket and paid the fee for the volunteership. I took care of the rest. My calling was guided. It was meant to be.

My father, poor old man, couldn't understand why I had wanted to fly to the middle of nowhere. According to a map on the immunization dr. 's office wall, it was the most diseased place on earth. He couldn't wrap his head around it, when I myself was not at my best. I think he knew deep down that this was something he may never understand. So, he gave me his blessing, and took me to get over twelve vaccinations for my trip. He loves me, I know.

I wonder what my mother would have thought?

On February 1, 2011, I flew from Los Angeles, California to Nairobi, Kenya. I landed late at night, and as I was flying over, I could see the land fires from tribal activity. Life was here. There was super-sonic electricity pulsing through my veins as we narrowed in on the motherland.

I landed and was greeted by my hosts, Lily and Dean. They were mom and dad to all of us volunteers and kids at camp. I was greeted by a family, and picked up in their personal van. I was immediately introduced to Wambui, who instantly became my sister. It was as if we were childhood siblings. We knew each other's souls. She was me, and I was her. Only in different worlds, separated by seas.

Three days into my trip, Wambui and I were at the market in Nairobi picking up vegetables for a dinner stalk, when my nose began to run uncontrollably. I started to feel a bit ill. I requested we go home so I could rest. Obviously, I thought, I was just jet lagged. When we got home, I popped a couple of Nyquil and fell fast asleep.

When I woke up about 5 hours later I was completely drenched in sweat and I couldn't move my muscles. I was almost paralyzed. I slithered out of my lower level bunk and made my way to Wambui. She looked horrified. I must have been ghost white and sweating like I was in a shower. She rushed downstairs to get her mother, who ran to me. Dean then picked me up, put me in his van, and drove me straight to the hospital.

I couldn't walk. I kind of limped and was mostly carried. My fever was so high I was blacking out. I don't remember a whole lot until I was revived. After what seemed like an eternity, and several rounds of blood testing, it was official. I had Malaria.

The doctor inquired as to why I hadn't come in sooner. He said that my entire system had been affected by now. My fever had been so high for so long. "That goddamn Nyquil," I thought. I slept right through all my vital warning signs. I was reprimanded. "Westerners and their quick fixes. pShh." Eye rolls came from the entire medical staff, and for the first time I truly felt American.

I just laid in my own sickness and pity, while barely making out my surroundings. My vision and consciousness were in and out. I barely remember the blood streaks on the concrete hospital walls, with the tripod light above my head. I also decided that, if this was my death, I was ok with it. If this was my time, well, then this was the way I wanted it to be.

"Is there anyone you would like to call?" the doctor asked me.

"Yes, my father." He is going to kill me, I thought.

The phone rang and he answered. I instantly began to cry, loud soulful "Im dyyyyyying," sort of tears. It's true, I was. But they were working on it. They knew I was going to be ok, technically, but *I* was really sure that this was my death.

"Daddy, I'm sick. I'm in the hospital, I've caught Malaria. I'm scared."

"Oh Doter." He said gently.

"You're going to be ok. I have spoken with your doctor. They say you came in very late for what stage it's in, but you're going to be fine. Take it easy, do what they say, and come home to me. I love you."

That was all I needed to hear and I was fine. I did make it. I pulled through after five days of blood transfusion and cleaning, it was one of the most painful medical encounters I have ever had. It was one hell of a process, but bless those Kenyans, they have their shit together.

As soon as I was released from the hospital, Lily and Dean insisted Wambui and I get away to the coast to relax a bit. Since I was just freshly cleaned, mosquitos wouldn't bother me for the following six months. I was immune for the time being. I grabbed Wambui, and off we went to Mombasa. It is a ten hour bus ride through the night to the coast of Ukunda, Diani Beach. Where the sand is white and the water is crystal clear.

The most beautiful place on earth.

It was February the 12th, 2011. We had arrived fine, but tired and a bit early. We had to sit and wait for a bit while we decided what to do with our time. That's when I met him. He came walking up the stairs in slow motion. I had never laid eyes on a man like this. He was conducting business as the manager of entertainment and guest pleasure for the hotel. He introduced himself with perfect eye contact and smiled so bright, I was blinded.

His name is Thabiti, in Kenyan this means, *'true man'*. He asked to be called Thabi for short. Thabi is a native to Kenya and speaks four languages. This man has a very large personality. I am without doubt that he was designed to make everyone, especially women, feel the way I did. Special. And it worked. Shortly after our brief introduction, Wambui and I were shown to our room. As soon as the door closed, I screamed with excitement.

"OMG! Wambui did you see that!?"

"Yah, gal, I saw it! Do you want him?"

"Yes, I want him!"

"Then, you shall have him." We giggled like young school girls, while holding hands, and jumping in a circle. We quickly changed into our bikinis to go out on a glass-bottom boat ride with some of the local boys. We found fun fast. We had bought outfits for this occasion, so we were dressed to the nines, and more often than not, we matched. After endless sun on a bottomless boat we headed inside, showered, pranced around, and then changed into our matching dinner gowns and attended our first feast together.

Thabi found us quickly, and invited himself to our table. My heart was pounding so quickly, I think I spit up a bit the first time I opened my mouth. We talked easily, the three of us. He stopped in the middle of one of his sentences, looked straight at me and said,

"You are one of the most beautiful women I have ever met, sorry to be rude, but I couldn't hold that in any longer." I must have turned bright red.

"You're kidding right?" I looked behind myself to make sure he was indeed talking to me. Wambui was giggling softly. She whispered, "I told you so."

"Well, thank you." I said calmly, I had relaxed. He made the first move, so it was on. I had yet to become comfortable with myself and still quite unsure of who I was, so making any move was not my thing. He invited us out for the evening, he would be our guide. Take us to the local bars where we could dance. We agreed eagerly! He left us to mingle with the other guests. We left to change yet again.

We went out to a beach bar…where the waves are the yard and the bar is covered by tall African grass, full of Germans, and some locals. This place was magic. We began drinking and dancing into the early hours of the morning. The night was full of laughter, fun, exploration, and excitement. Wambui was growing tired, and requested we return to our quarters. I agreed. He suggested I go home with him. Again, I agreed. We dropped her off and went back to his place.

It began with a subtle suggestion, "Do you feel like you need a shower?" he innocently inquired. Not so innocently, I thought. I was hesitant because I don't really like `sexy showers'. There isn't really anything sexy about two people in running water and *not* cleaning up. Nevertheless, I put my weird issues away and agreed to feel dirty and let him clean me up. He began by untying my sarong knot with his teeth, and pulling my panties down with his mouth. He traveled up my legs with his tongue, until he found what was between.

He began to send me off with intense pleasure. I had never received such incredible oral euphoria such as his. We moved to the bed, still dripping. He rubbed me down for a moment, then crawled on top, and entered into what I had thought was forbidden territory. I thought, "I really like this guy," and "where is this going?!" My head started butting into my vagina's business.

Before I could finish my thought, he had me screaming. I was screaming so loud we could hear the neighbors waking up. This lasted for hours. He didn't care about the noise, he kept saying, "Good, let them know I am king." In the morning, I woke up to him pressing his slacks for work and brewing coffee. He looked at me and said,

"You were making quite a bit of noise last night, princess. How do you feel?" I wasn't sure. Physically, I was still in euphoria. I had never made love with a man like him, an African man who is connected to the earth and to himself. A man who is of his own accord. I left his house, my favorite walk of shame ever. Down a small dirt road across from our resort. I tied my shirt and sauntered my way back to the room. Wambui answered the door with an ear-to-ear grin on her face.

"Sooo?" She inquired. I collapsed onto the bed face up and sighed a big sigh.

"I am in love," I said.

"Good, gal! It's a good thing! Let's go ride camels along the coast!" She casually said, and off we went!

Thabi and I would brush past each other, exchanging flirty smiles and secret winks. He made me feel special. I was already planning our wedding. We would have it here at the resort, I thought. Right where we met. We would have two children, and they would also know four languages, like their father. It was perfect. His affections only affirmed my delusional fantasies.

It was now February 14th, 2011. Wambui and I were to attend a special dinner, all made up for lovers, she and I were each other's dates. We slipped into our very best and incredibly coordinated gowns, we did our makeup fancy, and our hair was also styled. We looked ravishing! When we walked into the diner hall, silence fell upon every guest. All eyes were on us. We locked fingers and proceeded to our table.

Thabi came over to poke fun at the scene we made upon our entrance. "You girls really know how to put on a show, I see. Good job, you look amazing, both of you. Enjoy dinner. And Sophia, I will see you later." I knew he was coming for me. I just had to wait. Wambui and I thoroughly enjoyed our candlelit dinner. I was with my good friend and it was by far the best Valentine's Day I had experienced.

In the following three days, I would spend all my time with Thabi and Wambui. We explored the coast and just played around. We even extended our stay by three days so he and I wouldn't have to part just yet. When we finally did part, Thabi and I would keep our communication running daily, using Skype and email. It was working while I was in Africa, we were in love with each other, and still in the same time zone.

Thabi taught me things about myself that without my interaction with him I may still be struggling with. He had mentioned my health and said things like, *"You are only beautiful when you're not smoking."* He said that if I ever wanted to be taken seriously, I would have to take care of my body. No one hires a lazy person, and if you don't look after yourself who will. He said I was attractive enough, but he could tell I didn't eat right and I didn't spend even a minute a day at the gym. I was outraged! Only because he was right.

"I love you," he said, "you're going to make a fine wife. But I think you won't be ready for some time." I was furious. We had begun our descent before I had even left the continent. I wasn't quite ready to focus on myself in that way. I carried on my relationship with Thabi for three months from start to finish. We ended in May-ish. He decided I just wasn't the girl for him and so he let me go. I was ok with that. I did mourn the loss for some time, almost a year. My heart was broken.

However, not all was lost. My time in Africa was deeply enriching for many more reasons than self interest. I learned so much about humanity, economics, and geography. It was truly incredible. I had been working with the children for almost two months by the time I left in April of 2011. I learned so much about myself, about life, about what true happiness is. The children want for nothing, they are content with the beans and rice they receive, seriously.

I learned a little bit about motherhood, I decided I would never spoil my children with Western gimmicks and tricks. I want my

children to be as soulful as these children were. I learned that true
love is found in its densest quantities when it is between parents and
children. I felt it. I loved those kids and they loved me back. It was
an amazing experience. The most valuable lesson I learned somehow
also came at this time. I learned that no matter how your parents teach
you or mold you to become, the person that you are, ultimately, is up
to *you*. You decide who you will actually be.

I returned home and mourned for almost a month. I was culture
shocked upon my return. Life was big and wasteful, I had found
depth in my soul, and America no longer felt like home. My father
had never been happier to see me, he welcomed me home with open
arms. After I was done with my dramatic display of self-perpetuated
culture displacement, we sat down and talked about everything. We
discussed my future. I wanted to go back. I wanted to live there. I
wanted that life. I was serious.

He discouraged it, said I still had some growth to experience here,
and that I had made a promise to my boss. I needed to stick with it.
He also inquired about my weight. He was sure to say that no man
would want to marry me with a spare tire always hanging about my
waist. While I can acknowledge how harsh that is, it was interesting
to me that Thabiti's concern was from a professional stance and my
fathers was from a marital stance.

In any case, both could be validated or made to be void, the truth
of the matter was I needed to do something about my health. I was
getting older and I was beginning to show signs of trouble in my ag-
ing. So, I hired a personal trainer and kept working on cars at Grease
Monkey for the next year.

CHAPTER 13

Back To School

Noun: Time of year when you get new clothes.

January 19, 2012

> *Today, I am writing to you as my adult self, or close to it. I have issues: many thoughts race through my mind all at once. More often than not, I ponder the same thing over and over again. I just think about it a little differently each time. I want to see a new fact every time I re-open the subject. If I can't fully dissect something then, what, I ask you, is the point? I have become addicted to my own opinions and thoughts. I have become addicted to solitary behavior. I have a mild to severe case of social anxiety, and tend to be very awkward at times. I seem to be very talented when it comes to being awkward, then and only then do I seem to know just what to say. I haven't been a very good friend lately. I was supposed to go to Germany for my birthday, but at the last minute I freaked out and couldn't get on my plane. I decided to stay in California and spend some quality time with my nieces. I missed them. I stayed in San Francisco the day I was supposed to leave for Germany. Anthony had to work so I went on a bike ride with his friend Aaron instead, whom I hooked up with later that evening. Aaron made me feel like such*

a woman. A beautiful, sexy, powerful woman. I don't
have to tweak anything about my personality to be
around him. He didn't spoil me or cater to my being.
He treated me right. And, I wanted to fuck him, so I
did. Always, Sophia Nahlah Saber

Aaron was, at first, not very attractive to me. He was tall, but not
husband tall. Maybe six feet. His eyes were perfectly proportioned to
his face, which seemed disproportionate to the rest of his body. He
was a heavy cycler, so he was fit. We seemed to have the same way
of keeping our secrets from one another. We talked about our pasts
and why we were the way we were. But with him, I found myself
leaving out many important facts. I loop-holed my stories and lied
even. I wanted to continue to be the person that he adored, and as my
truth would have it, I feel some of my past is not so desirable for men.
However, I think we both seemed to understand the fact that possibly
we would never get the full story from one another. We exchanged
numbers and kept in touch over the next several weeks. I loved seeing his name on my phone screen. I left San Francisco for the city of
Angels, the city I love. I went to visit my best friend Wilona and my
goddaughter, to spend some time with friends and family.

January 22, 2012

Well. Hello! I'm sitting alone at a sushi bar on
Hollywood and Highland. I am alone, because I like
to be. Also, some recent self-realizations have come to
light. There are some things I have never noticed about
myself. I guess that's what friends are for. They are like
mirrors for your insides. I do not like who I see. My
behavior indicates lack of self respect, a severe need for
negative attention, and finally a sick addiction to love.
I'm not sure when all this started. I'm almost positive
it was shortly after I left Ice. I left that good girl be-
hind. I don't know if she will ever be back. I guess it's

true what they say, "Once a good girl goes bad, she's gone forever." I miss the cooking and the cleaning, the nurturing of a man, the back rubs, the sex, the laundry. Seriously, I miss doing a man's laundry. Speaking of Ice, we went hiking today. He has a new girlfriend who sings. He is finally where he wants to be and seems happy. I am happy for him. I do not wish for our return. I am so happy we are still amazingly close. We went hiking in Runyon Canyon with our second dog, Riley. Anyway, it was nice. Except, the uncomfortable thing about today was that Aaron was on my mind all day. I couldn't get it to stop. Like, what is he doing? And is he any good? He probably is. He is probably beautiful, smart, funny, and charming! All that jazz. Why would Aaron ever even give a second thought to me? I'm just wasting my thoughts on him. Who knows what he is up to. Sophia N. Saber

That couldn't have been further from what would actually happen. Aaron got a hold of me right away, and our correspondence began. We sent love letters in the mail and finally he called upon me. Asked to come and visit. I agreed. While Aaron and I were cooking up our new romance, my focus in life was more on my career. I had new plans and new ideas of where I wanted to take my life. It was high time I went back to school.

I loved working with my personal trainer, Jared. He became like an older brother to me, instantly. He was not only helping me understand my body better, but he was always listening to my problems. We were becoming great friends. I loved how my body was shaping up and also how he was someone I loved meeting up with and talking to. My interaction with him inspired me to follow in his footsteps. I enrolled at an accredited and accelerated school for sports medicine.

It was the perfect next step for me. In the meantime, I needed a GED to obtain an education from this accredited academy. I first researched paper mills. I didn't really want to go back to school, but

I needed to do something. I read online that if the school is caught with anyone who has a fake diploma or GED, they could lose their funding. So, out of politeness to them, I did it the right way. I began to study for my exam in November and passed it in December, just in time to finish enrolling for the Spring/Summer session.

For income, I had given up my pseudo passion for mechanics and found a more reasonable starting position working in a retirement home restaurant. It had been one straight year since the switch, and I had begun to build some real skills in the kitchen. I felt totally safe in all I was doing on the professional front. It was time for me to refocus on internal callings; like the one I had had since I was in fifth grade. We were introduced to a period in time in which I would discover my first ever female hero. Anne Frank. After reading her diary and learning her story, I was forever changed.

I was fascinated with the holocaust and WWII histories. I was completely inspired by her. I wrote in my diary like her and even felt trapped and doomed like her— but in a more American way, a psychological way and yet; we both still wrote about boys as an escape. I was inspired by her then, and the feeling never left me.

I felt I needed to walk in her footsteps, or as close as possible. I needed to be where she had been, and see what the scenery was like that inspired her words. I wanted to connect with that energy, and feel the horror they must have felt. I don't know why. I just did. I was feeling a calling to Germany to explore this history for myself. I booked the trip and made my plans.

I intended to visit Auschwitz, maybe sit in silence on the dirt, and pay my respects to my early ancestors. The plan was that the trip would last for two weeks in January, for my 27th birthday. I wanted to start a tradition of travel on my birthday. That year was Germany. I first made my way to San Fran to catch an international flight from SFO.

However, my travel plans would give me my first guttural pause. I stopped at my gate and went back to Anthony's house, interrupting my German plans. I completely gave up my whole flight and left. I was just starting to learn to listen to my gut no matter the expense. The expense this time was a refunded ticket and a rescheduled flight. I wasn't feeling it and I had to respect that. The plane didn't crash or anything, but I still had no regrets. I was happy to stay back in California and hang out with my friends, who I had missed so much. After all, that's when I met Aaron.

...

Back home, I had a monumental time in my life about to begin. My mother was gone and I now had to raise myself. I was clean, working, and beginning to travel. I was also returning to school, the best thing I had ever done for myself. My choices were starting to look so different. I was feeling all types of grown and sexy. GED'd the fuck up and walking into a legit classroom. This was *huge*, my official return to school.

I dyed my hair bright red for the term, I needed a change. Something to make me smile when I woke up. I wondered what my mom would have thought about my hair. I know what she would have said about school. *It wasn't church.* Maybe she would have liked my hair though? In any case, I walked into that classroom tall and proud. I found my spot up front. I knew that if I were to succeed in school I would have to pay extra special attention to the lessons. I always paid attention to other things, and nothing had changed.

Students piled in one after another, and we were introduced to who we would spend the next six months with. Every day, for six hours, from 9:00 am-3:00pm, four days a week. We were a small group of twelve. Introductions were short, but important. He sat right behind me. A few rows back, but right behind me, none-the-less. His name is Matt, Matthew Sparrow. He is the middle-aged man having a second wind in life. We all had diverse stories and that was his.

He is very handsome, well built, not husband tall, but taller than me. He wears braces, he is nearly forty, and he wears braces. I adore this immediately. They are not the invisible kind, they are the metal train track kind. He's rocking the fuck out of them. Matt and I immediately found each other. We found each other at a time when neither of us were really available, but we never acted like it. He was always snaring me into his traps. Constantly poking at me, paying me compliments and attention.

Matt had a girlfriend, but you couldn't tell by talking to him. I had a boyfriend out in Cali who was making plans to move to CO for me. Matt seemed to hate everything about relationships and family lifestyles. It was strange for me to be so attracted to this. Perhaps, I just needed someone to lean on during school, and in between texts from Aaron. Matt and I had a commonality, we were here for the same thing. School.

I was still rehabbing and finding my passion in life. Was personal training the answer?! I was determined to graduate no matter the answer to that question. He was going to help me. We found ourselves enjoying lunch together, everyday, at the same table, where he would eat the same thing. A dry chicken sandwich, cottage cheese, sweet potatoes and one piece of dove dark chocolate. The wrappers had little quotes on the inside, and everyday he would give me the wrapper. I don't like chocolate.

We became close friends, very close. With always a respectful distance, due to him having a girlfriend and me having a boyfriend. One night, however, he invited me to an art show. We walked and looked at the art. It was special, we went back to his place and began to fool around. He went down on me. I enjoyed every second, but it didn't go any further.

Aaron moved to CO around this time, and our relationship didn't last past August. Sure, he was suffocating me, but I was also burning a wick at both ends. I was suffocating myself. I didn't talk much about Aaron to Matt. I wanted to focus on him and his problems, not mine.

November 22, 2012

> *First off, Happy Thanksgiving. Second, wow, it's been*
> *so long since I have had the urge to write to you. But*
> *here it is, we meet again. My love life has always been*

an absolute mess. And I am at my worst this time.
His name is Matt. Up to this point, he is one of my
favorites. We have strong chemistry. And what sexual
fire burns between us. He loves me, I know he does.
He has experienced me in a natural setting. Seeing me
in class everyday is better than meeting me at a club.
He sees who I am day to day. I am sure of his love for
the real me, and not some fantasy he has come up with
for me to fit into. He is kind to me, winks at me, and
slaps my ass. I love making him think that I hate it. I
don't, I love that shit. Matt is an incredible man. He
is a fighter, but such a girl about it. I feel at times he
is slightly unaware of his actions. Like, a bit stupid in
the head, I think. But then, he is so fucking brilliant.
Matt could never have been a good friend, or even a
friend at all. There is something very unique about
our connection. I am sure of my feelings for this man.
I am totally 100% head over heels in love with that
man! He claims to be in love with me, or completely
falling in love with me. The other thing about Matt
is that he is totally in a committed relationship with a
47 year old woman. I believe she and Matt will remain
together forever. It's simple, easy, stable, and reliable.
She is for sure a real woman. Then there is me, the hot
red-headed tattooed chick. Who sits in front of him,
who fell in love with him simply because he paid me
attention. I'm just a pretty thing to look at, just a play
thing. A fun toy, I will never be her or that woman.
I'm just SNS.

Matt took me out that night after I wrote this entry. We went
back to his place and had sex. By "we had sex," I mean, he came in
two seconds and I held him. He was almost crying. Through his tears,
he was able to mutter some words, "Since I've aged, I don't know

what the problem is, I can't last very long or even get it up at all." I exercised nothing but patience and understanding. I held him.

Then he said, "If I would have known that you were going to react this way, I would have done this a long time ago." I was floored. Had he been lying to me this whole time about who he was?! I thought we weren't doing this because he had a girlfriend. This small sentence of his just changed so much for me in the two seconds it took him to utter the words. I called him out on it and he just talked in circles. I was too excited that I finally had my conquest, I didn't care. I knew somewhere it wasn't meant to be for us.

He told me he would break up with her over Thanksgiving. It didn't happen. He said he wanted to wait till after the holidays, he didn't want to put her through that. I agreed. It's graduation morning now, and we're waking up together. I have a ride, he has a laugh. I'm good at getting it up and keeping it up, he says. I'm becoming quite comfortable with my sexuality.

We take our Certified Personal Training license test together. We both passed. We had breakfast with my parents, who don't like him at all. They think I can do much better. "He already has a girlfriend, Sophia." My father says in one of the most disapproving tones I can recall for him. "He is too Hollywood for you anyway...does he even know if he has a soul?!" He finished muttering insult after insult till I walked away.

Anyway, my parents played nice and held their tongue at breakfast of any ill will they felt toward him for what they both saw coming. Afterwards, we went our separate ways because he was spending the day with his girlfriend, and they were attending our graduation together. I was so excited to finally be graduating from something so beneficial for my life, but I was in love and alone. The usual.

I wondered if it had to be the usual. Where was my mom's advice, she would have stopped me from all this *nonsense*, as she would have called it. "Sophia, boys will always be there. You have to put them on the back burner." God, if I had a nickel for everytime my mom said that sentence to me, I'd have millions. She would say it with so much passion, too. She really knew me, and now it was time for me to know myself and be more responsible. That's what she would have said to me.

Matt and his girlfriend showed up together, and I just kept reminding myself that I was the one riding him that morning. She was the one asking where he was. I liked it this way much better. She even shook my hand and smiled at me. I felt so guilty. She seemed like such a lovely lady, she even complimented my jacket. If she only knew, I thought. She would be devastated she had given so much of her time to such a fucking douche bag. Oh, well.

That night at the ceremony was my first graduation from an institution since the eighth grade. I gave a small speech about gratitude for education, second chances, and how I felt I was at the beginning of something very big. I made a muscle pun, but it didn't go over well. I was nervous and had never had any experience in public speaking, but I had something to say. Something I wanted to tell the audience and my mom, so I volunteered to give the speech. I wish she could have heard it.

I went home, beaming with self pride. I had really fuckin done it. I stuck with it and I graduated. I was something, more than the nothing I had been told I would be. I was now ready to pack for that rescheduled and well deserved trip to Germany. I flew out the very next day. Matt and I decided we would keep constant contact, with Skype calls and emails. It was the perfect graduation present to myself. When I arrived, I met up with my good friends from Kenya. I was excited to finally be answering my calling to history. This time my gut let me pass by the gate and fly overseas.

I arrived shortly before Christmas. Festive little villages were set up every ten feet or so. I would stop for glue vine and Nutella crepes every chance I could. I was loving the beer culture and harsh deep accents. Any interaction with a German felt like I was being yelled at and loved all in the same sentiment. It's like they were all screaming at me with the most pleasant expressions, very confusing.

I thought of Anne often, as I would walk the streets in random places. Wondering if she had been here, or there, or what she thought, and how she felt about German people in the 40s. I never really came up with any answers, just something I thought about constantly. She was my focus. I learned almost as soon as I landed, Auschwitz was off the table due to its location being in Poland. They say Americans make this mistake often, but no one actually books the flight first.

I was in luck though! Because what *is* in Germany was Bergen Belsen. This is the concentration camp north of Hamburg, where Anne and her sister Margot died, just three days before the camp's liberation. I was able to make the drive with my friends through the thick, wooded forest, on a two-way road, in the dim mist, on a cold winter day in Germany. I walked where she had walked. I saw the pages of her diary, and placed my hand on the mounds of dirt where her body might lie. I was deeply honored, and touched. What a serendipitous solution to my miscalculation.

After that, it was just historically driven tourism: the wall of berlin, the cold snow of Frankfurt, and my body's reaction to traveling. I was constantly feeling ill. I went one week complaining constantly of my sickness. My friend went and got me a pregnancy test just in case, I assured her there was no way I was pregnant.

I was pregnant. And it was Aaron's baby, for sure. While we had just split in August, we continued to fool around till late October. I was seeing both men at the same time. It gave me a sense of some sort of power. I played with fire, and now I was burning for it.

I was fucked, already two and a half months pregnant, and no desire to have this baby. Judge me if you will, but for as bad as I *do* want to be a mother, I do *not* want to have a baby daddy. Having that baby never even crossed my mind. At that moment, I wasn't thinking of my mother. I would not have gone to her for advice. I was crystal clear on what needed to happen. Thankfully the best part and most of the trip happened on the front end, so having to cut things short didn't feel so wrong.

When I returned home from the German clinic and found Matt on Skype, he jokingly asked, "So are you knocked up, or what?!" I began to sob. "OMG, you *are* pregnant. Is it Aarons?" He asked patiently. "Yes." I calmly stated. "And I am not having it. I will have to go in as soon as I get back." He nodded in support, and hardly said anything about the fact that I had been with Aaron that recently. I don't think he truly expected monogamy from me.

When I returned from Germany, on December 24th, 2012, I walked the most shameful walk of shame in my life, from my back door to the front door of my father's garage. I sat in his chair, our talking chair,

"Daddy, I'm pregnant."

"Oh yeah. I thought Matt couldn't have kids?"

"It's Aaron's," I said.

"I see, so what now, you're gonna be a mom finally?"

"No. I have scheduled an abortion for December 26." He held me. I don't think he fully agreed with my decision this time, but knew when my mind was made up there was no changing it. The abortion had little to no effect on my relationship with Matt. He was supportive and caring. He was also still in a relationship with her. He just could not break it off. By the time my birthday had rolled around, I had enough. I waited till the perfect moment to throw a fit about something ridiculous. I intended to break up with him without feeling the same guilt I had felt for Aaron. I just ended things so abruptly with little explanation, I thought the fact that he STILL had a girlfriend was explanation enough.

So, I let him go.

CHAPTER 14

The Personal Trainer

Noun:a fitness professional involved in exercise prescription and instruction.

I walked through the doors of the YMCA, smelling body odor and determination. This was a new chapter in my life, the beginning of a new career. My physical evolution was finally starting to take shape, and I was determined to keep it fit. I followed my friend, personal trainer, and mentor, Jared, from one gym to the next. He was now the fitness coordinator at the Y. He said he had an opening for me, so on this day, I was there to interview for the position of Certified Personal Trainer.

I took my time, making my way down the long hall to the back of the facility where the fitness area was. I found Jared's office, and had my interview. This was my first job as a professional, I was so excited. After we decided on a start date and shook hands, I took a look around the place. Walking slowly in and out of each room, picking up equipment, playing with it, smelling it, putting it back down. Then, back down the long hallway that separates the fitness area from the gymnasium. I thrust open the doors and a big gush of friendly, sporty air hit my face. And there he was.

Mitch, who could have been the brother of Eric from the Little Mermaid. I made my way up the stairs, to the running track. It gave me a birds eye view of the whole gym. I could see everything, especially him. Beams of light bounced from his muscular body, so brightly I forgot where I was for a moment. He was setting up hurdles for his young client. He's a leader, an alpha male, I immediately thought. I hadn't yet noticed the physical details, as much as the details of him in his role. He spoke with such authority and didn't take notice of me. He didn't even look my way as I was dramatically making an entrance. Like a weirdo, I watched him for some time, circling above him on the running track around the basketball courts. He was precise, serious, and engaging. I immediately wanted to be like him.

It would be another three months before I saw him again. After working at the Boulder Y for some time, I switched all my shifts to the facility where he was. Not for him, but because I liked the demographic better. This was the same Y I had grown up in. I could visit spots where Jim and I had sat painting pictures in day camp. Mitch, just happened to work there, as well.

After some time, I had seen him enough to notice his physicality. He was tall, and built like a man made for warfare. Much like the men from 300.. He had brown eyes that spoke softly. He carried himself with a conservative nature, and spoke like a well-educated man. He always wore his shirts tucked into his gym shorts, which screamed loudly, "I WENT TO PRIVATE SCHOOL." I knew that tuck.

He was like nothing or no one I had ever been interested in before. There was something in his personality that spoke to me. Something inside him was calling to something inside of me. I was determined to explore this calling.

June 13, 2013

> *We sent playful texts all day, which ended in a serious mature conversation of how we should go about our feelings. I like this guy already and know almost nothing about him. He would be a great father, super attractive. That is all.*

During our first bout of textual exchanges, we talked about how to operate at work together and still have a romantic involvement. I made it clear that I didn't want to be kissed unless he meant it. I learned from *the co-worker* that this situation is tricky and usually a bad idea. However, I felt I had matured some and he seemed mature enough that if things didn't work out, our careers would remain the most important thing to either of us and we would remain professional as well.

We scheduled a first date, which was quite lovely. He wanted to take me golfing, I had never been. When we arrived, there was a wedding going on, so romance filled the streams of summer air. I was no good at golfing. With the toddler-like patience I have for sports, he kindly let me just drive the cart and drink my beer. I was making him laugh as he was trying to play golf.

June 21ˢᵗ, 2013

> *He took me golfing in Longmont. Watching him play sports was enthralling, he was precise, accurate, and challenged. He let me drive the cart and drink my beer-garitas. Next, we went to Boulder Cafe and had dinner. We arrived at 8:00 ish and left around 11:30. It was a good conversation, he made me laugh. He is smart, quiet, attentive, and realistic. I was dying to dance, considering my day was rough, so we went to round midnight and danced for a bit. He is a great dancer! I hate dancing with doods and he was just amazing. I spent the night at his house, since I had to open the YMCA in the morning. Anyway, we kissed and rolled around a bit. I think we even took a shower...no sex. I could totally get used to this guy. He could be my rock.*

I enjoyed this type of attention, he didn't seem to care so much for the surface details, he seemed to be an observer and was reserved about himself. I liked this because it meant he didn't go on dates often or spread himself thin between women. This was attractive. Would my mom like him, I often wondered.

Our first date consisted of me watching him play sports, as did the second. I began to love watching him, observing him. I'm not going to lie, there was something strange about Mitch. I was at my peak curiosity. Still, I was searching to love and to be loved in return, so I was willing to give each man his fair chance. I wanted to fall for him. I had yet to understand who I was at this point. I kept believing that the *fairy tale* life was for me, and that having a story for my mother was still important. I kept thinking she would like him, maybe even more than I did. And that satisfied me somehow.

One day, I was on a floor shift and got a phone call from him at work. He said there was something he had to tell me before we continued. He was so apprehensive to tell me. He kept it from me for days, even keeping me out of his sight so as not to have to explain himself. I kept asking him for the details and reasons for his secrecy for the following three days. Finally, he broke, in a gentle conversation over the phone, he said this.

"I know up until now we haven't had much physical contact, and there is a reason for that." I was on the edge of my seat, with the office door closed and the blinds drawn, listening intently.

"I was in an accident when I was a kid, and I lost the whole of my right leg, and some use of my hips." There was a small pause from him and an elongated pause from me. Was he joking? How could I not have noticed? How has no one said anything? It took me a few seconds to swallow my disbelief. I had so many questions suddenly, and knew I couldn't ask any of them. Instead, I just asked if he was ok. He gave a kind of loose giggle, to let me know almost no one ever knows what to say.

"Yes, Sophia. I am ok, it happened when I was nine." We both laughed.

"Mitch, you're not just saying this so I will sleep with you are you?" That question was followed by the longest, most awkward pause of our conversations to date.

"Well, ugh- would that get you to sleep with me?" In the seconds following my word vomit, I realized what I had just asked out loud. Frantically, I responded.

"No, no. I mean, not that I care, I was just asking. I mean, can you… have sex?" I inquired, an attempt to move past the horror that just spewed from my mouth, and into the next scene of the same movie.

"Well, as a symptom of missing a limb, I have phantom pains that get pretty bad. It's a huge hindrance to my love life, it holds me back and I've never explored much of it."

In this instant I was in love. I was determined to get to know as much as I could about him. And somehow be a safe space for him to explore. I was so attracted to getting to know how his mind worked in conjunction with the failure of his body. I was gentle with him from this point on. I knew that he was not *the one*, yet I still allowed my heart to be open to him. Maybe there was something for him to gain from me. Maybe I from him? *Perhaps the universe brought us here for a reason,* my puny human brain forced me to believe.

By our third date, we were sleeping together. It was awkward and quick. He was insecure about the process, and I wasn't mature enough to handle the situation with much grace. Even when he kissed me on my mouth, it felt like too much connection, as if I were sinning. That's the part I liked and disliked, it just never quite felt right with him. As exciting as it was, it was for all the wrong reasons.

One night in the dark, we were fumbling with our clothes. He was less interested in me each time we met, and I was frustrated by this. How could he not be in love with me?! How could he not look at me like the woman of his dreams?! I was truly astounded.

Our relationship would only last another month. He had a way of making sex into this mechanical sport, like exercise. In retrospect he really was doing the best he could with what he had; still, there was no passion, no fireworks, no drama. He never went down on me; he seemed to have no interest in the pleasure of a woman. Just cut-throat penetrative sex, kind of get in get out vibes. Once we had both come to this conclusion, our encounter died down on its own, for whatever reason, leaving me heart broken.

I thought I could love him and I was hoping he could love me. That's just it, I needed to learn that not everyone was about love, but rather, the encounter, experience, or what could be taken or left behind. He had made it clear to me how deeply interested in psychology I had become., With what he brought out in me when his disability was discussed, and by how stimulated I had become, not only sexually but intellectually. All I knew at the time was that I wanted to know more. With that we let eachother go.

CHAPTER 15

The Spaghetti Dinner

Noun: The meal before he chased me down.

I had met him once at Mitch's house. We locked eyes for a brief moment, while being introduced to each other. I had no immediate interest in this young man. He was tall, thin, and overly bubbly, with the energy of a small child. He was anxious to go out and play pool with his then tall and beautiful girlfriend. Mitch and I were not having it. This was the first memory I have of him.

More than a few months passed before the next time his name would come up, Felix. Felix Winters. I was in the sports office at the Y, talking to one of the coordinators, a friend of Felix's that was more like a brother. I was telling him the woes regarding my website and new independent personal training company. Some of the things I struggled with happened to be professional skill sets held by Felix. His friend recommended I speak with him. He was a computer programmer and could help with the website.

I was hardly interested in that idea. However, as fate would have it, a few weeks later I ran into him at round-midnight while shooting some pool. We said hello, and I told him what was going on. He was more than happy to help, so we exchanged numbers. He called immediately, and the next day he came over. We sat around my computer and chatted and laughed. He showed me computer codes and how to track the monitoring of my website. I was amused by his intelligence, so was he.

He was easy to be around, and I knew that night there was

something between us. He was so different from his odd friend, with whom relations had ended two months prior to our meeting. He left my house that night with a very obvious yearning for me, one that I could not satiate. I was apprehensive of my new feelings for this familiar fellow. Yet, we had fun together, and after my last experience I was now craving this kind of connection. I wanted laughter and story telling and those were the two things he provided for me that evening.

In no time, we set a date to do something fun, not necessarily a *date* but it totally was. Clearly we were interested in each other, but I had yet to realize how close he and Mitch actually were. That following week he was my date to a live performance of "The Twilight Zone." Not to be confused with the ever trendy glitter vampires, no. This was the real deal, 1964 Rod Serling, "Twilight Zone."

It was a small town theater right up the street from my house. Literally, three blocks away, and in the 27 years I had lived there on and off, I had never been. I thought for sure he wasn't going to show up, his communication on the text had been a hit or miss all week. To my surprise and luck, he showed up. Looking ever so dapper in his man boots and fitted jeans. I liked his style. It was calming, confident, and just enough.

We watched the play with equal content and interest, not only in the play but in each other. I wanted so badly to reach over and grab his hand and place it on my leg, as I am sure he wanted just about the same. We had yet to explore what there was between us. As the play ended we decided the night was not yet over. We went back to my place and watched TV until 2:00 am. We then proceeded to order silver mine subs. He chewed his food quietly, and let me pick out what we would watch on the TV. I found a certain sweetness in this type of behavior. A sweetness that he did not seem to naturally possess, it was as if he was being sweet just for me. I certainly appreciated it after all I had gone through. I just wanted to be treated nicely.

We fell asleep next to each other making careful movements so as not to get too close. We were still "just friends." He slept on the outside of the bed, keeping his hands to himself. Yet somehow, I had found my way into his arms. We woke up the next morning around 10:00 am, and without a second thought in my head, I threw the covers up, started jumping around shouting, and barking like a lost puppy.

"Let's go eat! Let's go eat!" I could feel how his child-like energy seemed to revive my soul. I was awake, not just for the day but for life, and I wanted Mexican food! We made the two and a half minute trek up the street to the Mexican breakfast restaurant. We ordered our food and read the paper, comfortably ignoring each other at the table, as if we had been married for years. We played the crossword in our own version and shared lots of laughter. He was a problem solver, a riddler, and a thinker. I really liked this. He challenged my brain with his off-beat pattern of communication (that I understood like a second language), and his curiosity about life and all the mysteries within. He became irresistible to me in this short time.

We walked home holding hands and playing the love tap game with each other. What happened next seemed as though it was written right into the script, like a scene from the movies where they want each other so bad they can't keep their clothes on. There was snow on the ground as we raced for the last 30 seconds. I fumbled with the code to my house door knob, but eventually I got us in. We were kissing in a gust of teenage like passion, eyes closed, rolling our bodies along the hallway wall (down steps, no less!). Books falling from the shelves, shirts torn, pants unzipped, breathing heavier, hands all over, exploring each other's bits and pieces.

My panties seemed to just melt away in the heat between us. The next time I could catch my breath, he was inside me. The pillows were behind my head as it hit the wall over and over. I was no longer even on earth. I was floating so high I couldn't see the ground. I heard him and he heard me and for that moment we were together in space. We finished together. We lay there naked in silence- out of breath and slightly confused. It was like 11:37 am (but who was looking at the clock?). What had just happened was not a drunken mistake or a quick hit.

We had connected throughout the night. The combination of our three speed dates had led us here to this moment. Were we ready for the commitment sex brings? For the questions, like, who is this person? Do I really want him inside me? How is his integrity, is he honest? Will he communicate with me after? Do I want to communicate with him after? Why did I just sleep with him without knowing these things? I was again confused by my behavior. My brain was again, butting into the business of my vagina.

But I trust love and by this point, welcomed the experience. You never know when you're going to get your next ah-ha moment, or big chance at a major love. Most things that interest you at some level deserve a chance, I say. Our escapade would last only three short months. Felix was young, and I was ready (or so I thought I was) for something a bit more serious. I knew I was looking to have kids soon, and he was not on that page. That didn't stop us from sharing an array of sweet moments.

What I had learned from Mitch was that not every situation is meant for love. Though I knew I loved Felix already, I also knew he didn't love me back. That doesn't mean I didn't drag that shit out. One night I went to his house, still with the snow on the ground. He happened to live with his mother at this time, which I gladly accepted. I missed my own mother terribly, and welcomed that interaction. I was making spaghetti and salad while I also did both of their dishes.

While I was cooking, we began to have a disagreement. The words began to gain weight like an out of shape bodybuilder, what once looked like a strong bond between he and I, had begun to wither away at this moment.

"I just don't know if I could ever love you." He calmly said to me, "Why not?"

"I know what you and Mitch had. I know that it is over and it wasn't much to begin with, but it will always be in the back of my mind that you slept with him."

"But, Felix, this is something you clearly knew about from the beginning. How can this just now be an issue?!"

In my mind he was confused. While he wanted me, the friendship he had with Mitch was far more important than having a relationship with me. I get it, I do. So I finished cooking his dinner and left in a silent feminine fury. I cried the whole way home, tears so big I had to pull my car over and just let it out. My heart was broken. He was such a jerk! Yet, the only person I was mad at was me. I should have known, how could I not see this coming?!

I made it home safely, 35 long minutes later, still crying. I rushed down my bedroom stairs and threw myself into my plushy bed and continued sobbing. My clothes were still on, and my room was pitch dark with complete silence. My phone rang over and over "Call from Felix, call from Felix." My phone said in a pre-siri voice. I ignored it all, "Just let him go." I keep whispering to myself. Of course, he'll want me back, I just walked out. Men like to scramble after you leave or calmly dump them. "He doesn't *truly* love you. He loves himself" I kept whispering.

I've found men chase you if you leave, but if given the chance they would have left you first. It's a sad little game we play, most of the time it works, but not this time, Mr. Winters not this time. You will have to chase me down! All I have ever wanted is to be wanted. Chase me down if I leave, show me you care and you want me. Is that too much to ask? A little crazy? Perhaps.

Look, I didn't run to be chased. I ran because he told me to. When he said to my face that he could never love me, that's my cue. My phone kept ringing. It wouldn't quit, so I answered in an angry, silent-tear-ridden voice.

"What?"

"Sophia, where are you?"

"Where do you think I am Felix? I am at home."

"Stay there, I'm on my way." My heart sank. I sat straight up in the dark and thought. Oh my god, he *is* chasing me, he *is* the one. I hung up without responding, like they do in the movies. It seemed fitting to our scripted story thus far. Fifteen seconds later he was knocking at my back door. I texted him that it was open. I was determined to let him find me miserable in the dark, with runny mascara and a dramatically broken heart. I knew it was not his fault, but I wanted him to really want me. I knew if I presented to him a case in which he had to problem solve, I could hold onto him just a little bit longer.

He knelt down beside my bed and told me how his mother had come home seconds after I left, inquiring as to who washed the dishes and cooked dinner? When he told her what happened, she told him to come after me. That Mitch didn't matter if it was love, and to go after her, she said. So, he came.

We laid there quietly and began to make love, he promptly left after and I thought nothing of it. I knew he wasn't lying about forgetting his work clothes. Who thinks of packing an overnight bag when you're chasing a woman down?

Christmas was next, and I was moving into my own apartment. After four years of living with my father and brother, it was time for me to move out. I figured this would help Felix and I maybe have a chance at something with some privacy. It didn't.

He continued to deal with hardship and ridicule from his friends for messing with the left overs of his best friend. It was getting harder and harder for him to look me in the eye and to share affection. He was turning his passion for me into resentment, and it went from bad to worse.

During the Christmas season, he attended a plethora of ugly sweater parties and I went to a few with him. He came home from Denver one night and had this to share with me about the party.

"There was this girl there at the bar and we were talking." I knew right away that this wasn't going to be a "I hit on a girl" or a "girl hit on me story," Felix didn't have those. He always had inquisitions about people and always had something interesting to say. So I was curious about this girl and was already aware that I was in for a surprise ending.

"She says she has a boyfriend, but she's thinking about breaking up with him."

"Ok, why?" I asked, pretending to be at the edge of my seat.

"She says he never went to college and she is afraid they won't have much in common. So, what do you think about that?" He asked me, as if we're on a hidden camera show. So, here I am waiting for Regis to pop out with a mic, and all I can think about is how his tone and curiosity in my answer showed what he really was asking me. Or rather, telling me.

I quickly realized, there was no bar and there was no girl. *We* were his scenario. Felix was very well educated, with his Bachelors in All-Knowing-Genius and a Doctorate in Fact Vomit. It was obvious my level of education was now his dissatisfying way out. He wanted a woman that wanted more, and I did want more. I wanted to be a wife and a mother. Is there a degree in that? To answer his question, I said.

"She is stupid to judge a man based on academic knowledge, which is the cheapest knowledge the planet and stars have to offer." He wasn't buying it, he was going to find a way out no matter what. Eventually I let go of Felix. In his absence I was left with the rumination of his academic sentiment. I found myself curious about what the big fuss was. I mixed his sentiment with the interest in psychology I had just found to enroll at the Community College. I began my First semester on January 21st, 2013. I began school, again, and soared right into the next chapter.

CHAPTER 16

You&ve Got Mail

AOL: *Fastest way to get butterflies in the 90's*

He came to me at a time in my life where I had just begun a pact of celibacy, and serious academic pursuits. I had decided that in order for me to really find myself I needed to be alone, both emotionally and sexually. I had been through what I thought was enough exploration, and what was also my last year of being 20 something. Now was the time to figure my shit out.

On the day we met, there were certain energies I was focusing on. Specifically, my new found love for academia. I had signed up for my first semester at a community college at the ripe age of 29. I decided to take psychology, philosophy, and an English class. When he walked into my office, I was writing my first ever college paper on a book called, *To Kill a Mockingbird*. There was a knock on my door, and like many times before, I had assumed he was a gym member about to ask for guidance. "Yes, sir." I looked at him seriously. "Are you Sophia?" The tone in his voice sent shivers throughout my body. I knew I had never felt power like this. When he spoke my name for the first time, I truly understood its meaning. I felt all the victory inside me stand at rearing attention. "Yes." I must have said firmly. "Do you know John?" He asked quickly.

It was John that brought us together. This stranger had told me that John approached him in the men's locker room, claiming that he had to meet me. He brushed him off, and then again was urged just to meet me. It took him some time to decide on a 'yes,' but he found it, and he found me.

There we were in my office, alone. I had pulled the chair out from under the desk so fast, it was still spinning when he caught it. I was completely captivated with his tone and earthy nature. He lived in truth, and I could feel it. I was behaving sternly. I was the cute personal trainer in the office, so this was nothing new. Except this time, dear stranger, I invited you in. I wanted you there, because it truly felt like you wanted to be there. This feeling of being wanted or just having someone take genuine interest was nice and warm. I could see it in your eyes, as you told me of your life and your lineage.

I found it so sexy and attractive that you took your ancestry seriously enough to trace thousands of miles of your ancestral pilgrimage by foot. I wasn't letting any of the gooey I felt inside show on the outside. The conversation continued to flow perfectly. We had a beautiful resonance, as he had mentioned to me in one of our first exchanges. "What are you studying to be?" He asked curiously. "A sex therapist." I said boldly. He kind of giggled and asked, "Why?"

This was one of the first times I had so clearly and honestly expressed my passion without doubt in my voice. I felt as though I could speak freely. I felt powerful and honest. I could feel the good in me by talking to him. Talking about being in school was something new to me. I was, after all, a first generation college student and honestly had no idea what I was doing. I just knew it was better than the life I had been previously leading. So, I was beyond enthusiastic to converse on the topic.

After I finished my romanticized sex therapist explanation, he voiced his stance on academia and how he was in a revolt against his studies. He had climbed the ladder so high that he couldn't remember what he was climbing it for. I completely admired his trust in life, and in that moment I wanted to be him. I wanted to climb the same ladder he had been climbing. How odd that he entered my life right when I was looking at all the opportunities in my fresh pursuit of academics.

He left the room for just a second to go grab me a copy of his book. I was not big on reading (yet), my initial thought was, "Great, that's all I need, some hot stranger handing me another book I will never read." Though, that's what I thought, I actually *did* read his book and I <u>loved</u> it. Every word, every moment, and every thought. His writing style and how engaging he was. He had captivated and inspired me wholly. We talked for almost an hour and a half, then it was time for him to go explore the mountains. It was our lucky day. our last chance to meet, and we got it.

I walked down the hallway next to him, it was my favorite part. I felt so tall and beautiful, the walls were passing me in slow motion and I wanted to lock my fingers with his. I wanted to reach up to embrace him and never let go. These were very strong urges I was fighting. Alas, I shook his hand and we parted ways; but immediately united through email.

February 22, 2014

> *Dear Stranger,*
>
> *You took me by complete surprise today. I was not expecting any of the elements that continued to unfold as we exchanged words, ideas, and hopes. The most surprising of these elements was how much like me you sound, or how much like you I sound (as you are older), either way. It was refreshing and a confirmation that I am indeed on the right path. It was nice to feel as though I could speak freely. I thought it rather adorable how you stopped yourself from a "Jesus speech" because I gave a subtle hint I may or may not be a christian. I was just making sure you weren't. It was nice to feel cared for, even if it was just for that moment.*
>
> *I felt a strange vibration the first time you said my name. I responded professionally, but it felt wrong. Look, I don't know who you are or why you happened to cross my path. I am acknowledging that I did feel*

something when you were near me and for some time
now after you left. I would have waited until I finished
your book, but I'm on page 27 and my friends will
be here any minute now to drag me off for a night of
drunken tom-foolery and ridiculousness (I hope). It
is my last year of these inexcusably tasteless wastes
of night. Anyway, here is my way of saying I liked
you too, and in whatever capacity, I'd like to keep in
touch. -Sophia

It only took him a few hours to respond. I was in shock. His response was lengthy, honest, and open. Inviting me to interact with something we both seemed to want to explore. Our interaction then heightened, and over the next month we would share over 73 e-mails, exchanging ideas, hopes, fears, dreams, laughter, and complete resonance.

One month into our correspondence, he invited me to Skype with him. It felt like our relationship was moving to the next phase, when you know you want to spend more time with this one person. Our letters were of a romantic nature most often, and were the foundation upon which our communication and understanding of one another came.

However, I am not reluctant to realize that there were signs of him not being ready to be so deeply involved with someone. He was not in a time and space that would allow for us to have a tangible relationship and this fact was tearing him apart regarding his feelings toward me.

Two months had passed since we met and our communications were daily. I could feel myself falling for him. One night, while on Skype, I was rambling about something (as usual). Explaining that it's hard for me to accept love due to my history and experiences with it. Then, immediately, I panicked because it sounded to me that I had alluded to an idea that *he* loved me. I stopped myself in the middle of my sentence "I'm not saying *you* love me, I'm just saying I feel..." "But, I *do* love you." He interrupted quickly.

No moment in my life had ever impacted my soul so thoroughly. The truth in his words, the freedom in his expression of them. It let me know that this was his truth. I felt his love for me. I was in shock, and there was a long pause. I tried my best to continue the conversation with him, but I was so excited inside I couldn't concentrate. I wanted to do a thousand arm pumps, and also wanted him there with me, perhaps inside me.

On that note, due to my celibate practice, we rarely spoke of sex. As a matter of fact, he would ask permission to think about me and to connect with me sexually when he would masturbate. It was incredibly respectful. I found this irresistible and it just heightened our connection. After three months of heavy correspondence and shared moments in love. I suggested that he come see me for a few days. By that time, he was ending his travels and had reached his final destination, and quite noticeably our correspondence had changed. He had changed.

I offered to fly him out here, since I knew that money may be an issue for him being in the wandering position he was in. The justification for my proposal was that I just didn't want money to be a hindrance, or the reason we couldn't explore this love, which was priceless. He responded quickly. "No, now is not the time. I feel if we were to meet, it would be intense. Furthermore, I don't want to lead you on. I don't want you to think that this is going somewhere. Or that you are the only woman I want to see."

To be honest, I was expecting the *no* and would have been surprised at a *yes*. I was prepared to continue our correspondence for however long it took him to decide he had a *yes* to see me. It was the second part that tore my heart right out of my chest. I felt the internal bleeding killing me slowly as his words of rejection kept pouring out of his mouth like tap water accidentally left on. I felt my eyes welling with tears of confusion, but no anger. I still loved him at that moment.

We talked about how this connection of ours was new and hard to navigate for both of us. We had both been in love before, but this was new, on a completely different plane of romance. We understood one another completely and were different enough to still be totally amused by each other. I knew about his previous relationships, and how he had suffered infidelity. I knew the whole time he was still healing from that, and also, that he had not let go of that woman. I could hear the sadness of loss and rejection in his voice every time he spoke of her. I chose to believe what I wanted; which was that he would eventually get over it.

I wasted no time in "breaking our bond." The next day I broke my celibacy with my artist friend. I spoke to him the next day and had, again, wasted no time in telling him out right that I had broken my celibacy. While I was feeling good about the time I spent with my artist friend and my decision to come out of my celibacy, his response made me feel as if it were a mistake. "But, it's only been three days. How could you?" He said sadly.

All I could offer was silence, I wasn't sure how to feel. He had a look of sheer disappointment on his face, and I will never forget those eyes. I had never seen them so sad, the image burned into my brain like a branding. He was hurt, and I was feeling responsible for that. But more so, he seemed to be disappointed in the fact that I had broken the promise I had made to myself. No matter how well-worded my justification was, he was just not having it. I didn't hear from him for a few days and when I did hear from him again, he let me know that he, too, had been with another woman. It was official our bond was broken and he and I were a thing of the past.

"Good!" I said in a high pitched teary-eyed voice. "I know you probably needed it, knowing what you went through with your ex. It's important." My reaction, however well played, was a cover for the sheer devastation that I felt. My stomach was churning in knots and I felt sick. The images of him with another woman were putrid and almost unbearable. After we ended our conversation, I spent the rest of the afternoon in tears. I knew I was at fault for everything that had crashed and burned between us. If only I had exercised patience, if only I had loved him the way he deserved to be loved. If only I had rejected fear and pronounced love, we would not be here. My after thoughts were in vain as he was already gone from my life, and my heart.

Though, not all was lost. Through my correspondence with him, I found bits of myself. Who I am and what I truly want in life. Through honest communication with someone who I wanted to be more like, I was able to convey what I truly wanted without hiding or lying to myself. I had never found that in life, that is, until now. As I was sifting through our many lengthy email passages, I found this letter and it touched me the way I hoped it touched him.

February 28, 2014

> *Dear Stranger,*
>
> *I am happy to share how I feel You have awakened something in me. You deserve to know. I was going to wait until I had some more time to respond, however something you said has been bothering me all day. If I somehow led you to believe I currently have children, I am sorry. I have none to date. I speak so completely maternal at times, because more than being a writer or a sex therapist, or a trainer..model..mechanic, what-ever. I want to be a mother. But I take parenthood perhaps the most seriously of all life's adventures. I have been very careful to not have any children before I know it's time. Even then, I'm still 70/30 on actually having birth children. I have my reservation for many reasons. If I were to claim some divine purpose in my life, it would be to break the cycle I was born into. My mission in life is to have a daughter and love her wholeheartedly. To be the first woman from my family to treat my daughter right and teach her how to love her daughter and so on and so forth. Everything else is minuscule, in comparison. Again, for me, that is a far time from now. Parenthood scares the crap out of me. It*

is the loudest call, one that never dies. Every moment,
every lesson, every corner I turn is inevitably to pass
that wisdom on to my children. In essence, everything
I do is for them. I can't wait to meet them. =) But,
no, to answer your question, I do not have any children
currently. Just wanted to clear that up. -Sophia

When I read those words again, it came to me all at once. I wanted to be a mother. The most powerful of all my callings is motherhood, yet no matter what, I have been unsuccessful in reaching this goal. Just reading these words was enough to remind me to get back on my path and not to worry too much about such an uncertain loss of love.

Not too long after the dramatic ending to our virtual connection, our dear stranger wrote me an email. He had responded (to an initial mail sent by me) by telling me that he was in a relationship with another woman, and he had chosen to give his heart 100% to that relationship. I respected that. He continued to say that he still dreamt about me and had fleeting fantasies of being with me again. However, he made it clear that he had no intentions of ever being with me and that he would never come for me. Hearing those words at that time devastated me. Who had I given my heart to and why does this keep happening?! I loved him. I really loved him. He didn't need to say those words to me. We could have kept our friendship.

But seriously, fuck him. Fuck him, for thinking so highly of himself that he thought I was sitting around waiting for him. I didn't *need* him, I *wanted* him. Wants are easier to walk away from than needs. I didn't dream about him or have fleeting fantasies. I was hurt, sure, but I was focused on my own journey. Academia was still a daunting new force in my life and still focusing on finding ground to build a foundation to support a healthier love life and motherhood. So, what of my artist friend and celibacy I brushed over? Great question, but that's a whole chapter of its own.

100 Days

Noun: the state of abstaining from marriage and sexual relations

He was whispering in my ear how good this pussy was. He kept kissing me on the mouth while he slowly and passionately penetrated my, now 100 days celibate, soul and body. It was like I had never seen a boy before. He knew just how to touch me, he knew just what to say. Then again he already knew me so well, how could he not.

My sexual awareness and self confidence had dramatically improved in the short 100 days I had been celibate. The goal I set my mind to, to be more secure in my sexuality, had been achieved. I was ready to get back out there. I had a new view on me, and a new view on men.

I never found fault with men. They seem to be mysterious and sensitive creatures, which lends itself to the forgiveness of their baffling stupidity. It's forgivable, as well, because I found that women also suffer from such fatal conditions as entitlement. As if we are entitled to the love of men because we love them (or because we consensually sleep with them). I had a fresh perspective on the binary genders. Not perfect, or correct, just fresh.

I wanted to explore these concepts deeper. What was it that drove *me* to push a man into commitment? What was it in me that needed this, and how did I obtain what I wanted using the abilities and tools I was equipped with as a woman. What exactly am I looking for?

These were questions I could now answer in the vacuum of no sex. I wanted a man to grow old with, a man who was the best thing

I could ever do for my children, a man with the integrity of a god, who had the honesty of a child, the work ethic of a machine, with empathy for earth and all creatures abiding within. Most importantly though— I wanted a man that wanted me back.

So, I ask myself now, what kind of woman would this kind of man possibly be seeking? She is: supportive with suggestive honesty, she has motivation to be an inspiration for her children, and is prepared to raise them well. He will be looking for a woman to be the best thing he ever did for his children. She should encourage laughter and lightness for him, she should work diligently in her role as a professional and a domestic engineer.

The list continued. I went through every trait I wanted in him, and countered it with a trait that would compliment him as a woman. This exercise helped me lay out my desires in clarity and set my intentions with more stability. I could stop falling for men just because they paid me attention, or whatever small reasoning I would come up with. I needed to strengthen my own foundation. Not having examples is no excuse. I felt as though I was saving myself from another potential addiction. Now, when I look in the mirror, I see a grown, slightly educated, beautiful, healthy woman. If I want to choose to engage with a man in relations, I will. As soon as someone decides that it's no longer a tangible relationship, then fuck it...in the words of Jay- Z "Onto the next one."

However, that is much easier said than done. It's not like I had just been scarfing down men like bacon for breakfast. No, just the opposite. I had been engaging in love. Moving onto the next one is never easy. Withdrawing is not easy, but I can start my practice now, and someday it will be easy. Easy or not, I had managed to move on from each one. In fact I moved on so many times, that it had brought me here, to myself, to my celibacy, and to breaking my celibacy. A second chance.

100 days into my celibacy...

I got a message from him, my artist friend. "I'm in town for the weekend, if you're not busy we could meet up for lunch or something?" I thought nothing of it, as we have been good friends since I was live-in /dating his best friend DJ Ice. After the break up with Ice, I had remained friends with not only him, but some of the band mates. Whenever I was where they were, or they were wherever I was, we made it a point to meet up. This time was no different. "No, I'm not busy." "Well, I'm in town for some business. I have a show at the ogden you can come check out tonight." "I'd love to."

I drove the distance and arrived late. I met him at his hotel and we left immediately to get some food before the show. We laughed and reminisced, talked about raw fish, and how I only eat pretend sushi to look as cool as my more adventurous friends whenever we go out. He poked fun at my "circa 1945" cell phone, and my "burner" car, as he calls it. He got me all caught up on his latest projects, successes, and failures. I wouldn't even call it mild flirting, we were friends and it felt good, natural and safe to be around him.

Arriving at the venue, I could tell we were only there to show face, so our time was short. What happened to us next was out of character. I grabbed his hand as he led me through the crowds of people. He kept looking back to make sure I was still smiling. Watching him in his environment, interacting with people and laughing, shaking their hands, and being the man they came to see. Something about this in that moment was almost irresistible to me.

Still, *I mustn't,* I thought. We've been friends too long, I dated his best friend for almost five years, and I'm celibate. It's the alcohol. Just as soon as the thought entered my head, it all began, my heart reacted to my thoughts and energy was released from me. The music was playing loudly in the background, the openers had started playing, he was the headliner of course. He walked up behind me and slid his arms around my waist, we began to sway to the music in unison. I knew then that what I was feeling was mutual.

He kissed my ear softly and smiled at me politely. I found it quite soothing. I hadn't yet decided that breaking my celibacy would be the best option for me at this point. So, I pulled away. We went back to just hand holding, and then mild flirting. I watched him from backstage as I had hundreds of times before, this time the lights hit him differently, his mouth moved differently, his words hit my ears differently, and I was ready to go back home with him.

Upon our arrival back at the hotel, there was no pressure for sex. Not even a hint. We were sitting face to face, and I was just about to leave. Before I could get my next sentence out, he looked at me and said with such sincerity and tranquility in his voice. "I want you to sit on my face." There was a long shocked pause from my end, no one had ever said those words to me. My initial reaction was to fight it.

"I'm celibate, I can't do this." I said. "So am I, I don't want anything more from you than this." I was saying no, but in my mind I was already naked and comfortably seated on his mouth. He made me feel safe, wanted, and beautiful. And even though, after all these years of knowing each other, and the words "I love you" had never been spewed, in this moment I could feel his love and admiration for me.

I gave in, not to him, but to myself. I now wanted what he was offering. As far as my celibacy, this wasn't a mistake. This was the universe's way of providing a safe environment and a powerful man to help me. I didn't even bother with dressing after my shower, I ran to the bed completely naked and excited for what was about to happen. As quickly as I could climb under the covers, he took me in his arms and kissed me passionately. He asked if I was ready, then slid his hand down between my breasts, down my abdomen, and between my legs, opening them for the answer to his question. "Yah, you're ready," he smirked.

He put me on top of him, facing the opposite direction. My motion was motivated by love and mutual respect. I was completely enjoying what I was doing to him, and what he was doing to me. Hearing him moan gave me such pleasure, I always knew I was a giver. But no one had ever received it quite like him. The intensity of what he was doing to me was dramatically increasing. I was un-aware of time and space at this point. I could feel my body beginning to quiver. When I was able to concentrate on myself, I couldn't tell where his mouth began and my wetness stopped, he was completely submerged in me.

I had never felt pleasure this way. While I was enjoying the moment, I couldn't help but to ask myself a few questions. Why was this different from any time before? Was it him or me? Or us together? Or was it different this time because, in my short 100 days of loving myself, I had succeeded. I love me? I know more about who I am and what I want. He was what I wanted, this situation was completely mutual. Equal desire from both persons. It was both of us. I knew we were not meant to be together in the sense of marriage or kids, but we were meant to be together at that moment.

Before either of us could come to a screeching halt in our oral activities, he grabbed me and threw me to my back on the bed. He opened my legs and took what was his. He kissed me on my mouth while he slowly and passionately made love to my body and soul. While deep inside me, he continued whispering in my ear how good this pussy was.

CHAPTER 18

Thank you, next

The song I want them to play while the credits roll.

January 15, 2015

Hey, you. Today is the day I have been waiting for my whole life. Thirty is here, staring me between the eyes. Asking questions like, are you happy? Are you satisfied? Is the life you have the one you always wanted? Are you in love? Do you still miss your mom? And, what's next?

I'll answer these questions in a little bit, but for now I am waking up slowly in my hotel room in central Cambodia, Siem Reap. I have just finished nearly a month of backpacking through Vietnam. I began my adventure in Northern Hanoi, caught a train to Hue and spent some time there, then onto Ho Chi Minh (Saigon). I am spending time with myself, away from America. I can't shake the feeling that I do not belong in that atmosphere, however reality would have it a whole other way. I came here to start writing my book. To gain perspective, to heal my wounds, to celebrate me. My time in Vietnam has relaxed me, it has reminded me that when something out of the norm happens, if you go with it, your heart is better protected from anger, frustration and stress.

I crossed the border into Cambodia three days ago, and have been around to see the temples at Angkor Wat and the floating villages down south. I have found enlightenment in these sights and adventures. The world is so much bigger than my drama, it really lends itself to a fresh perspective alignment. It goes without saying, but there is some disappointment in these places, which are sacred grounds for the Buddhist. It seems at times these places are nothing more than grand tourism at its finest. Just a bunch of dick heads walking around being loud, snapping selfies, and looking for the next dollar beer. Maybe I'm only bitter because I am one of them also.

I will get a tattoo today to celebrate my 30th. Then I will fly onward to Bangkok. I will spend some time there and then fly home. Writing the beginning of my story has reminded me of so many painful parts of my past that I would otherwise like to erase from my memory. Some I will be glad I wrote down to remember for all time. I am reminded that I am still not a mother. It is still so unclear to me at this point, how or when I will become one, and that is ok. I am reminded to welcome the journey, as well.

I must not fail to recognize that on this day, I am not missing any love. I have left the anger I felt toward my mother for leaving me so suddenly five years ago, and I love her and every memory of her, even the bad ones. It all made me who I am today. My father loves me. We have spent a good amount of time communicating on Skype this trip, and to feel my father's pride is what gives validation to my existence.

My sister and my nieces miss me. Our love is deep and strong, I am lucky. My younger brother, his baby mama, and their son Kaidon. It's all good, we all love. My co-workers at the YMCA, my kitchen family, they all mean so much to me. My new/old Colorado friends, my friends in Cali, my ride or die chicks. It's for life…. I got them, they got me.

Shit, now that I am looking at all that I do have, I forget what I don't. And in that lies the key to happiness. The antidote to longing is gratefulness. I am happy and content. I am one lucky person. I am beautiful, healthy, and alive to be writing this. Against all odds, I've crawled out of the darkest corners and am making my way toward the light. I am a fuckn' college student, who saw that coming?!

Hell yes, I am ready to be turning thirty. Waking up in my Cambodian paradise hotel room. The music from the temples is playing loudly for the whole city to participate in. The chanting of the monks is rather loud. I awaken slowly to check my iPad, any messages? Any messages from him?

"Good morning darling, oh shiiit happy birthday!" He says. I smile softly and doze back off. I am content just to hear from him. Someone has grabbed my heart while I have been here. No surprise. I had just checked into my third hostel in Ho Chi Minh City, I was sitting on the bottom bunk which was not mine, talking to another resident. We were laughing at the tourism of the city and she was explaining to me her woes of Cambodia. Then he walked in.

He was loud, aggressive, and Scottish. Very Scottish. He spoke abruptly to me, not even noticing me, just another traveling woman sitting on his bed. He was rushing around to go to some pool party. The more he spoke, the more ensnared I was becoming, fighting every urge to be interested in who he was. I kept telling myself over and over, I have had enough of this shit. I'm not here for this. Immediately, it's fuck him and his gorgeous face and impeccable dressing attire. Fuck his perfect voice. And fuck me.

I never seem to listen to myself, even when I know that I know better. I began complaining about not having anything to do. He looked at me and said, "Well, you won't get anything done just sitting there, now will ya Lass?" Sarcasm? Omg, I didn't even know him and he was sarcastic. Then it all began, the slow motion. His movements began to call to me and every cell in my body was standing at attention. I wanted him, I at least had to get to know him, something was here. He was leaving and I was beginning to panic. I had one night in Saigon and he was leaving. How am I going to find my way around this? I wanted to know who he was. I wanted to know everything about him. Right then, right there.

I began to pick up empty beer bottles lying around the room randomly, to call his attention to my boredom. That didn't work. He just found some more trash for me to carry on my way out. This was going to be challenging. I positioned myself out front, right where he was fixing his motorbike before he left.

"What are your plans today?" He calls out as he shines a tool with a dirty car rag.

'Finally!' I thought I had him.

"I don't know, I'm bored of exploring the same thing in every city, I want something different."

"Hire a motorbike and see the country."

His response infuriated me. LOOK AT ME! Dammit! He wouldn't. My friend from the hostel came down from upstairs and it turned out they were going somewhere together. I was instantly jealous. I was pretending to be so nonchalant, but every cell inside me was vibrating faster than I could keep up with. I was losing him. I hadn't had the chance to get to know him, I couldn't let that happen. Right before I was about to give up he said,

"Well, we're just going to a pool party, you can come with us if you want. I can fit two on my bike." Praise baby Jesus! I thought. "Do I have time to change?" "Sure thing, don't take too long, we're wait-ing!" I quickly changed from nothing to something, grabbed some sunglasses, and ran back downstairs. I hopped on the bike behind my friend and off we went.

This place was amazing. We crawled our way to the top of a sky-scraper, which had a very American style pool party happening on the rooftop. It looked like a scene from a 60's glam magazine. I was impressed, and so was my friend. The boys offered us drinks and we found a cozy spot on some bright orange couch cushions by the water.

At first, we stared blankly at each other's faces, then we fell into groups. My friend and his friend in one group, and he and I in the other. We spent hours talking poolside. He talked consistently. I mean, if he could be inside your head he would talk for you. He loves to talk, and is very good at it. The tone of his voice indicated wisdom and age.

He didn't speak nonsense, if it wasn't legit he wouldn't say it. I like that. There was no small talk with this man. He jumped right into the deep end with me. I knew the most intimate details of his life within hours of knowing him. After he had finished telling me the 'worst of the worst,' as he put it, he claimed he was so nervous about how much he had opened up, that he had to take a nervous piss. I found this so endearing. I could tell that our interaction was new for him, he had never felt this comfortable with a woman.

I was totally relaxed, this was all I had wanted, I wanted to know him and I was getting my way. I feel at home falling in love. Looking at possibilities, calculating compatibility. We both had tattoos, we both smoked weed, we were both rough around the edges with extremely big hearts, he was perfect for this moment.

He taught business English to Vietnamese students. He had two daughters, and loves them and their mother the way a man should. We continued our conversation for nearly three hours. I don't even remember getting a word in. I was just tangled up in his life, in his story. Finally— a man who was sharing with me all his secrets, in complete honesty and without me even having to ask.

We had been ignoring our friends the whole time, and realized we should get back to them. We made plans to return home, change, and go out for dinner and drinks. We had yet to decide our true feelings for one another. We kept it friendly. I acted as though everything he told me didn't matter. It didn't. His past was his past. I was more interested in his present.

We went out for dinner, and my stomach was very bothered. Of course, we all mutually decided on spicy fish food, that or fried spiders, or maybe even some dog soup. I was devastated. But I've always had stomach issues and I know when to resort to simple foods. I ordered plain white steamed rice. I was good, after all, at pretending to eat the fishy foods when I go out. He noticed my game plan and wouldn't allow it. "You MUST eat more than rice for dinner!" he demanded. "No. Rice is all I want, thank you."

We ate, laughed, and drank our way till the late hours of the evening. Then the four of us parted ways. I had been bugging him to take me out on his bike, to show me the city, the real city, not just the tourist trap. He was hesitant, just like all his moves toward me. Hesitant to let me be so close to him. I was persistent. The other two had fallen asleep and now was my opportunity. "Take me out on your bike, pleeeeeease?!" I had pulled out the big guns, batting my big, beautiful eyes innocently, my bashful smile, my subtle arm touch. He could see me, all of me, inside me, and outside me. He liked it. All of it. His fight was in vain, I had won that battle before it had even begun.

He drove me around the city on the back of his bike for hours, showing me all seven districts of the city and explaining how they all cooperate with one another. His old apartment, his new desired one, his favorite places, bridges, lights, restaurants. He showed it all to me. I held him. I sat closely, my legs straddled him perfectly and we fit together well; he was tall, husband tall.

It was past midnight and the city was still crawling the same as it did during the mid-day hours. There was no difference. We parked the bike to grab a drink and to walk around a bit. I wanted to grab his hand, but he grabbed mine instead. I felt safe, and somehow loved. I asked him in a moment of silence, "So, whose bed are we sleeping in tonight? Mine or yours?" Mine was the bed above his, this was just my way of gauging his reaction. There was *so* much hesitation. His brain was racing, his heart began to pace, and I just watched him squirm calmly. I had just offered myself to him sexually and he was actually hesitant! This was adorable to me. "Mine, I suppose." Ha! I *suppose*. "Ok, then shall we retire?"

I wanted him inside me. I wanted to feel him. When we got home, we laid together in the room for a moment. Pondered for a second about getting our own private space, but then decided against it. Instead, we built a fort around the bottom bunk and explored each other's bodies. his hands were on my thighs, running up my torso, he was spooning me, and I was comfortable within his embrace. He began to slide his hand into my panties. I turned to face him. We kissed and his hands moved from my thighs to my face. He was passionate. Genuine, and longing for the same love I have been longing for. We were longing for each other. He was hesitant to make love with me.

We were rushing something beautiful, or I was at least. I can take responsibility for that.

Now, he was inside me, on top of me, our eyes locked falling into each other's souls. He pulled out without finishing, and whispered in my ear, "I just want to hold you." We only have hours to know each other, I thought, and he just wants to cupcake. I felt no fear with him. I felt only safety and calmness. I wondered how much of it was him and how much of that calmness was from me?

He knew almost nothing about me. Just the tid-bits I had shared throughout the evening. He just knew my essence, how I made him feel, and what we had in that moment. I woke in the morning, surrounded by his embrace. I whispered in my morning voice, "I will never see you again." he pulled me closer and said, "Well, at least if your book makes you famous, I can say I slept with you." HA! True.

His response was funny, witty, just the laugh I needed. It was my first time being this aggressive and going for what I wanted. He was what I wanted. I was finally seeing a more powerful side of my sexuality. I was finally owning my shit. He sent me away in the van on my way to Cambodia. Saying goodbye to him was hard. I was so emotional, like I was leaving someone I had been with my whole life. Right before I got in the van, he yelled to me,

"Sophia. You best be on the ready. I'm coming for ya and I like my eggs poached soft, yah?!" I smiled and sat in the van alone. Feeling his essence with me, I traveled through the night, crossing the border into the Kingdom of Cambodia, ready for whatever was next. I sat with all my gratitude for what had happened and acknowledged the bitterness I felt at having to once again let it go. I just wanted to focus on the part that felt good and so that's what I did. The next morning I woke up to his texts still reaching for me, and I am still reaching for more. Hell yeah, I'm ready for 30.

Happy 30th Birthday to me.
Love Always, Sophia Nahlah Saber

EPILOGUE

Two Thousand Twenty-Four

After beating down that monster in the mirror, I found a path to peace. The iceberg of stillness inside me that I had barely met at the end of this story, is what I had been searching for in others, in vices, and in the darkness. I had to kiss a lot of frogs before I realized I didn't even want a prince. I'd rather skip rocks on the water, I'd rather read books and travel than write about love, or the pursuit of it. I am learning to let love flow in and out and up and down and go however it may want to go.

After reading my story, learning that I'm both the villain and the victor is a horse pill to swallow, yet here I am, tummy full. Many of the mistakes I made in my early adult life mirrored those of my mother, and had I known some of her secrets, perhaps I could have avoided some pitfalls. These are the stories of my core memories, of the void that was before me as I am. These are the stories my daughter will come to know of who her mother was before she was her mother; granting her a knowledge about her recent history to give her better tools to predict her own future.

Writing this has cleared my insides from harboring guilt, anger, or confusion. I have had to reopen old wounds many times with different adults watching over as I healed multiple layers. I have no regrets and I would live through it all again, just to be able to live to tell.

I've made it my art, sometimes painting beautiful masterpieces and sometimes wondering if a toddler could have done better. I'm left with nothing but gratitude, especially to all the men on these pages who shared with me their time, attention and energy. One taught me love, one taught me patience and one almost made me a mother. Life is beautiful, and it's a powerful, transcendental time to be alive. To have the ability to observe and record a life lived. What an incredible seat to have.

ACKNOWLEDGEMENTS

First and foremost, I thank my higher power, my daydreams. My thoughts about a future me that drove a present me to be better than the past me. Thank you.

To my therapist and her husband, thank you.

To my editor who understood the assignment, thank you.

To the countless Family and friends who have been listening to me say: "My book is almost finished" for the past 10 years, thank you.

To anyone who reads these words, your attention to my story empowers me. Thank you.

Printed in the United States
by Baker & Taylor Publisher Services